GRANDMA'S
on the
GO

A *single mom and her* *passel of kids hit the road* *with guts and gusto*

Hannibal Books
P.O. Box 461592
Garland, TX 75046

www.hannibalbooks.com

Published by
Hannibal Books
PO Box 461592
Garland, TX 75046-1592

Library of Congress Control Number: 2003115281
ISBN 0-929292-73-1

TO ORDER ADDITIONAL COPIES, SEE PAGE 173

Dedicated
to

my father,
for passing on his Gypsy genes;
my mother,
for her loving concern
for her gallivanting daughter;

my 12 children,
for having the courage
to accompany their mother
through storms, deserts, and 26 states;

my God,
for giving me patience, perseverance,
and a prayer life to follow my dreams.

"As for me and my household
we will serve the Lord."
Joshua 24:15

Acknowledgements

Grateful thanks to:

Verna and Arthur Wesihampel—parents who reared me in a Christian home

My children—Cherilyn, Colleen, Grace, Phillip, Christina, Joanna, Joe, Nick, Roy, Cora, Darrell, and Chris

First Baptist Church, Channelview, TX

Teresa Cox, babysitter and friend

Brother Alan Weishampel, pastor of Murray Street Baptist Church, Lake Charles, LA, and his congregation

Bonnie and Carol Dowden and their Mexican ministry

Members of Campers on Mission, who demonstrate a labor of love "as we go"

Mission Service Corps volunteers, who follow "wherever He leads"

New Jersey Writing Project directors Dr. Joyce A. Carroll and Edward Wilson, for teaching writing skills and encouraging their application

Wanda and Brett Stoninger—Christian friends who introduced me to Hannibal Books

Louis and Kay Moore—sharp-eyed editors who made this book possible

Table of Contents

Appendices

Part One

Two Feet and a Tent

ONE

Over the River and Through the Woods

My sweet, 80-year-old mother overheard that I was planning yet another trip. She pronounced me crazy. My oldest daughter had less kind remarks about my sanity. Not deterred, I have spread out my maps and started making to-do lists.

So what prompts a reasonably sane, single grandmother to "hit the road"?

"On the Mark"

Actually it's all my dad's fault, despite the fact that I was reared in a typical, 1950's suburb by city-slicker parents. From my dad, I had inherited a recessive adventurer's gene. He took my mother tent-camping in Canada on their honeymoon in 1940. She survived and continued to humor him. He, in turn, provided her with middle-class suburbia.

Memories of our family camping adventures are mostly restricted to faded, black-and-white photos. Daddy, grinning, posed with his hand on top of a tremendously heavy, canvas tent tied on the roof of an old, wood-sided stationwagon. Mother stands amid the clutter: Coleman stove, lantern, canvas cots, iceboxes, suitcases, and assorted boxes of kitchen paraphernalia. Her flowered dress with white, Peter-Pan collar and black leather flats worn with nylons reflects the notion that this is not going to be a primitive vacation. Nor will she get a vacation from being a homemaker.

Little brother, Alan, about three years old, is climbing on everything. I was about five. Our German shepherd, Pal, and I hang our heads out of the car windows.

I vividly recall zigzagging down the original entrance ramp into Carlsbad Caverns to be awed by stalagmites (the mighty mites go up, remember?) and stalactites ("tites" hang down and hold "tite"). I walked the entire, Big Room tour, while my brother—the big baby—got carried piggy back.

We carried a canvas water bag on the car window when we crossed the desert in Arizona on a trip to Los Angles. On the return trip our favorite uncle snuggled on the back seat with us and created a story of a family of mice. That story lasted hundreds of miles.

Garner State Park, Texas, had a dance pavilion built by the Civilian Conservation Corps. There I learned to dance on Daddy's feet to the tinny sound of the nickel jukebox. We swam and played in the icy rapids of the Frio River. Mother donned slacks and joined us to climb the mountain high above the beautiful rapids. She and I slid on the seat of our pants back down the steep trail.

"Get Set"

To make certain that I was properly socialized, during first grade Mother enrolled me in Blue Birds. In due time I flew up to Camp Fire Girls. Our meetings didn't have much to do with camping. We mostly played and made things. I was nine and very much a tomboy the summer Mother signed me up for one week of summer camp at Camp Niwana.

I was not happy. I was not social; I was sure I would hate it. I wanted to stay home and build forts in the woods with my brother and his friends.

The camp was far from primitive. We slept on old Army bunk beds in a large, screened bunk house that was attached to the chow hall. A separate shower house had cold water, not enough shower curtains, and Daddy long-legs.

Red mud lined the bottom of the swimming hole and turned swimsuits rusty. We made cute, crafty stuff, swam, canoed, and took hikes. During quiet time after lunch, I discovered Nancy Drew and the Hardy Boys on a lone shelf in the bunk house. I loved them.

We went on a Snipe hunt and made progressive stew. After dark, off in the woods, some of the counselors built a fire and cooked ground beef in a huge Dutch oven. We campers hiked by flashlight to the campfire and added something to the pot: a cut-up potato, onion, a can of beans, corn, or tomatoes. We waited restlessly, sitting on scratchy, fallen logs, slapping at mosquitoes, and singing silly songs. When our stew was ready, each camper's portion was ladled in her tin bowl. Delicious! Apples were cored, filled with raisins, butter, and brown sugar, wrapped in foil, and buried in the coals to bake while we stared at the stars. What a way to end an adventurous day!

I was hooked on camping!

"Go!"

I returned to Niwana as a Junior Counselor after my 16th birthday. With the help of a Senior Counselor, I had 12 pre-teen girls under my supervision in a new, screened cabin on the edge of the woods. Each week-end we said "good-bye" to favorites and those we were glad to see go and anticipated new arrivals. Now I led Snipe hunts and night hikes to the graveyard.

On Sundays, after breakfast, the entire camp dressed in Navy shorts and white, button-front cotton shirts wrinkled from the suitcase. We formed lines by the cabins and hiked in silent reverence past the misty lake into the secret, sacred woods. Up and down small ravines on twisting trails, we followed the older staff members. Stopping on the breast of a hill, we peered down into a deep gully. A huge, moss-hung oak tree clung to the opposite bank. Its massive, exposed roots hugged the steep slope. Ferns and wild violets were tucked between great, curving roots. Bright streams of morning sunlight filtered through the high, dense canopy. Moss hung, like dry gray icicles, from thigh-thick branches.

Campers and staff sat down on the bank, while opposite us, the Senior Counselors perched candles on the majestic roots and climbed on them to stand before us. Morning songbirds provided a background for our singing. In this awe-inspiring setting, even the toughest girl participated in a chapel service. On the return hike, no one was willing to be the first to break the reverence. Chapel at camp left such a lasting impression that throughout my life, I've felt a special respect for God's Creation.

A visiting forest ranger took us on a nature hike and pulled leaves off of a thin tree with shaggy bark. It was called a prickly ash. He explained how pioneers had chewed the leaves to deaden toothache pain. Then he encouraged the brave ones to try chewing one of the leaves of this "toothache" tree. It numbed my gums.

On the Fourth of July, someone borrowed a horse; I rode through the camp at daylight blowing a bugle, yelling, "The British are coming!" Sleepy little girls in baby-doll pajamas stumbled out of their cabins asking, "Who are the British?"

One morning the grounds maintenance man, mowing with a tractor, ran over a cottontail rabbit's nest, frightening off the mother rabbit and scrapping the skin off the backs of three baby bunnies. He brought the babies to the nurse, who suggested I try to save them. She gave me some antibiotic ointment to put on their backs day and night. The camp director made a special trip into town for doll bottles, which were filled with diluted, canned milk.

Counselors and campers took turns feeding the babies during the day. I had the night shift. To the amazement of the forest ranger, they all survived, to be released at the end of the summer.

On the last night of each session, tradition called for a wishing ceremony. At twilight the girls solemnly carried a paper plate and an unlighted candle from the chow hall. Their long lines snaked down and around the edge of the small lake. Drumming, Indian chants, camp songs, and short speeches set the mood. We counselors lit the girls' candles. Each girl silently stuck the candle to the paper plate and gently pushed it, and her wish to return, onto the lake. The twinkling flames reflected in the waters were hypnotic. With another counselor I was privileged to take a canoe out to retrieve, by the light of the moon, all the burned out candles and paper plates.

My candlelit wishes to return were answered. The following summer I returned as a fully paid Senior Counselor. The summer after, I was on the staff of a different camp.

So what makes this reasonably sane single mom repeatedly "hit the road"?

Perhaps it was the Paul Revere ride. In the foreword to *American Journeys* Bern Keating says, "Paul Revere's ride across the countryside . . . exemplified what has become the American genius: the itching foot, the willingness to take to the road for whatever reason, be it freedom, exploration, riches or a restless spirit."[1]

I consider my self adventurous, although cautious, and challenged by change and the demand for self-reliance.

I am inspired by English biologist Thomas H. Huxley, "Try to learn something about everything, and everything about something."[2]

Let my stories challenge your adventurous spirit. Join me "On the Road Again."

[1]*American Journeys: An Anthology of Travel in the United States.* E.D. Bennett, ed. (Convent Station, NJ: TravelVision, 1975).

[2]On his memorial stone in St. Marylebone Cemetery, London.

Part Two

Tenting on Wheels

TWO

Tenting

My camping and travel adventures were interspersed with marriage, the birth of two daughters, divorce, and college. Determined to be all I could be, I earned a bachelor's degree in art education, began a teaching career, remarried, divorced, earned a master's degree, adopted 10 kids as a single parent, and then earned a doctorate in education.

My kids were an excellent excuse for camping with the family and with Boy Scouts and Girls Scouts. As my grown kids moved away, they provided grandkids—another incentive and excuse to travel.

The best way to explain senior rebellion is with flashbacks.

"I am not looking forward to tomorrow", I wrote in my journal. Primitive camping with a herd of Cub Scouts did not look as inviting as it did 40 years ago. This senior citizen wasn't excited about sleeping on the ground in a two-person, military pup tent with my nine-year-old, Chris, who doesn't like to brush his teeth and is too shy to shower.

We would contend with mosquitoes, South Texas's 100-percent humidity, and a forecast for temperature in the low 100's, (nighttime lows in the 80's).

But I had made a commitment to help chaperone; my pride wouldn't let me back out.

I packed insect repellent, sunscreen, foam pad and sleeping bag, mosquito netting, extra clothes, rain gear, boots, flashlight, and plenty of vitamins. Everything had to be securely stashed in plastic trash bags. The forecast also included rain. We had enough equipment for a safari. Fortunately we were not scheduled to backpack.

Am I in good enough shape (overweight and blind as mole without my contact lenses or glasses) to keep up with these boys? I recalled impetuous, primitive camping with the Girl Scouts 20 years ago, and accepted the challenge. This was one of those age-denial experiences. And besides, all the exercise would be good for me.

A truck hauled our gear to a trail leading to the campsite— 15 canvas tents scattered around a clearing. Several sweaty trips were required to move gear to tent. The tent flaps were down to hide that musty canvas smell. As the tent flaps were pulled back, creepy crawlies scuttled through the cracks in the plank floor. I quickly opened both ends of the tent to air it out and tried to create order out of my stuff.

Camping would be primitive, alright, but this I could take. Then I visited the pit toilet latrine. It was a two-holer with a sheet metal urinal—home to wasps. It had no door. I threw a beach towel over the plank at the top of the door opening. It covered the top half. At least it was obvious someone was in there. I hoped.

Then we had the swim test. Everyone who wanted to swim or go boating had to take a swim test. The boys changed, slapped towels at each other, and hopped on one foot then the other on the hot cement.

I sucked in my stomach, wrapped up in a huge beach towel and joined a line of 20 to 30 pre-teen boys, 8 to 10 adult men in various states of aging, trying to suck in their bellies. Most of them were more out of shape than I. A few brave mothers joined us. I didn't feel quite so conspicuous, even though I was the only gray head.

Macho water-safety instructors, flexing their adolescent muscles, gave instructions to jump in and swim once around the perimeter of the pool, then swim the back stroke, and finally survival float for an eternity. I made it! I earned my swimmers' card! Chris, a good swimmer, was not impressed.

Following after the boys was great exercise. I'm sure a pedometer would have shown at least 10 miles of hiking a day. We all sweated gallons. Exhausting, but more fun than a treadmill. For dinner we had a salad-and-fruit bar—also hamburger steak, mashed potatoes and gravy, green beans, rolls, and ice cream. Diet? What diet? I had to maintain my strength.

After supper was a two-mile hike to the campfire. And a two-mile return hike after dark. We fearless leaders drug up the rear, our bodies drooped and feet hurt. A miracle! A latrine just for ladies! What a relief. It even had a bare light bulb, better than none. Chris had decided to bunk with John, so I had a bit more room. My cot sagged. Under the mosquito netting, I was hot, sticky, and stinky with repellent. The monsters, not deterred, buzzed and crashed into the netting.

I dozed into sweaty delirium and reminisced.

In my reminiscing, I remember my oldest daughters—Cheri, the tomboy, and "little miss" Colleen—advancing through Brownie Scouts to Junior Girl Scouts. I was happy as an assistant leader. Then they became Cadet Scouts without a leader. I got drafted and nearly drowned becoming certified as a canoe instructor.

The troop backpacked with other Scouts in the Big Thicket of East Texas, a swampy jungle. Know-it-all Cheri led the troop, while Colleen was cooperative but prissy. The day was forecast to be great for hiking. Partly cloudy and cool changed as rapidly as only Texas weather can to freezing drizzle interspersed with thunderstorms. My sleeping bag was as inadequate as the small nylon tent flapping in the wind. I was tempted to untie the tent flaps and let the marauding raccoons in for warmth, but I feared that if I touched the tent walls, they would leak.

The girls, snuggled up together in their tent, didn't complain until it was time to get up and start a fire. Colleen, the cold-natured one, begged for my rain poncho and began to gather tinder. Cheri pouted that she didn't feel like searching for firewood. Only a senior leader had the foresight to put firewood in her tent. Griping and all that practice making teepee fires paid off. Hot chocolate never tasted so good!

I dozed.

One a.m., Chris and John crept up to my tent and whispered, "There's a raccoon under our cots." So what are you doing outside? "The mosquitoes are biting." So where is your netting and repellent? I gave Chris my bottle of repellent and insisted they go back to face the "raccoon". They argued that they couldn't go back because they didn't know where their flashlights were. Then how did you get over here? I gave them my flashlight to go find one of theirs and to search for critters. Just as I dozed off, they returned my light and reluctantly promised to go back to their tent.

I was actually looking forward to the next day. Activities, including canoeing, were scheduled just for adult leaders. I had not been in a canoe in far too many years and questioned whether canoeing was like riding a bike, where you don't forget how.

Back in my Girl Scout days, I had passed the Red Cross canoe instructors course and had taught my troop canoeing with borrowed canoes on the Trinity River. Cheri begged for us to do an overnight on the river. She prodded the other girls into agreeing. Colleen reluctantly went along.

Our canoe adventure began early on a clear, cloudless fall morning. We launched five canoes with two other adults and seven girls, two to a canoe, and gear evenly stowed in each. Our destination downstream was 12 miles as the crow flies, 18 miles by car, and probably 30 miles by watercourse. The water was high enough to provide a swift current downstream. We would have sandbars on which to rest and camp. Saturday was ideal—

cool and breezy. We made rapid progress past virgin forests teeming with birds. After the canoe paddlers jostled for position, racing subsided to peaceful paddling. Only the occasional drift and sunken stumps broke our steady stroking rhythm.

With about an hour until nightfall, we pulled up on a high sandbank, beached the canoes, and pitched our tents. The girls built a fire for cooking supper and for the prospect of ghost stories. A few high clouds had been rapidly floating overhead in the afternoon and now began to build into a thunderhead. Raindrops began to splatter the sand, hurrying us to store everything in the tents. I insisted my tentmates dig a ditch around the tent and erect a rain fly.

During the night rain began. Hard rain. The lower walls of the tent began to leak; the edges of the floor got wet. We yelled encouragement to the other campers, determining that their bodies were damp but not their spirits.

Breakfast was whatever we could find that wasn't too damp and that didn't need heating. Those of us who had remembered ponchos put them on and fashioned rain gear for the others out of large trash bags. We rolled up wet tents, emptied water out of the canoes, and stowed the wet gear. Each canoe team found something with which to bail. Continuing down the river in a light drizzle, paddling and bailing, our spirits rose with the lifting of the clouds.

There! Above the tree tops. A rooftop! Civilization! Our aching arms resumed paddling in earnest toward a sandy shore that held the imprint of human feet. We beached the canoes. Several girls went with one of the adults to spy out the land, hopeful of finding someone home who would let them use the phone.

Strangers welcomed us like neighbors, or castaways, while we waited impatiently for our support team with trailers.

Pre-dawn, and my neighbor was making coffee. A few adults have been stirred by the aroma. I hurried to the latrine.

The Cub Scouts were finally asleep, now that it was time to get up. Raccoons had been in Chris's tent. Torn candy wrappers evidenced their guilt, both the coons' and the boys'.

We adults had a class in Dutch-oven cooking. Our first assignment was to make a charcoal chimney out of a No. 10 can. First both ends of the can were removed. Using a punch type can opener, holes were punched around the rim on one end. A 12" square of chicken wire was stuffed into the end of the can just above the holes. Two holes (opposite each other) were punched near the other rim for the insertion of a wire coat hanger for a handle. To use, a wad of newspaper or dryer lint was lightly stuffed into the can on top of the chicken wire. Charcoal was added. I lit the paper through the bottom holes. Air entering the holes fed the fire, which lit and heated the charcoal. I then added more charcoal. When the charcoal was white hot, I poured most of it on the grill and set my Dutch Oven on top of it; then I put more white-hot charcoal on the oven lid.

Most any casserole-type dish could be cooked in a Dutch oven. The all-time Scout favorite was cobbler. A large can of pie filling was dumped into the pot and topped with dry cake mix, onto which dabs of butter were dropped. Peaches with yellow cake, apple pie filling with spice, or my favorite—cherry with chocolate. Yumm!

For an easy dinner we browned slices of link sausage and sliced potatoes, added a little water, covered, and baked until tender. Then we added a can of Ranch beans. A Girl Scout treat for breakfast was browned bulk sausage, cubed potatoes, and eggs scrambled together and served on tortillas with cheese or salsa.

Another Girl Scout treat that I never saw the Boy Scouts make was biscuit-on-a-stick. First you scraped the bark off of a long, green stick. You make biscuit dough from a dry mix. Kneed the dough into a long, thick roll; wrap the dough around the stick, beginning at the tip and winding it down the stick, carefully sealing the edges together. Heat the roll over coals until the dough is browned. Carefully remove the cooked roll from the stick; fill the center with butter, jelly or honey.

Both Boy and Girl Scouts liked Silver Turtles. On a doubled piece of foil I placed a piece of boneless chicken or hamburger patty, slices of potato, onion slices, and carrot strips. Season and fold up the foil into a packet. Place on the coals for 10 minutes. Turn over and cook for another 10. When you eat off the foil, you have no pans to wash!

The highlight of my Cub Scout camping-reminiscence trip was canoeing. I soloed on a calm lake, under a clear cloudless sky. The canoe was responsive to my whims to investigate quiet inlets along the wooded shore. Although my sore knees and shoulders were gentle reminders that I was not as fit as I once was, I learned that canoeing is like riding a bike—you don't forget the basics.

THREE

Tenting on Wheels

Too soon my oldest daughters outgrew Scouting and home and were on their own, I had adopted Nick, now seven, and had two foster kids—Grace and Simon, both 16. We no longer were involved in Girl Scouts, but camping still called to me. Giving in to age, I gave in to a camping trailer.

I answered an advertisement for a Coleman pop-up trailer. The camper was set up in the owner's yard. The roof was up, the beds pulled out, and the levelers were down. We bombarded the owner with questions. He demonstrated putting it down for towing and setting it up again. He was so helpful that I wondered if he was overanxious to make the sale.

He coached us to push in the beds and lower the roof. Then he showed us how to set up. First unlock the front and back at the roof. Crank up the roof. Pull out the beds, level the trailer, and set in the door. We practiced making the table into a bed, examined the propane stove, small sink, and chemical port-a-potty. The kids crawled on the beds. With the table lowered between two bench seats it could sleep six very friendly people. We made a deal.

The seller oversaw our attempts to break camp and dismantle the thing. Then he showed me how to hitch up to my van and hook up the lights. He waved my check as we pulled out of his driveway to adventure.

The following weekend we took a shake-down trip to a nearby park. Drinking water was carried in gallon milk jugs because the water storage tanks had not been sanitized and I

Hi Jeannie

As I read this
book I thought
of you.
Love
Aunt P.

didn't know how. I was scared of the propane stove and pre-ferred cooking over an open fire anyway. An ice chest solved refrigeration needs. We all agreed that the port-a-potty would be for extreme emergencies only!

Danger in Daingerfield

Our first real camping trip with the trailer was to Daingerfield State Park in northeast Texas. The kids had a great time swimming in the cool lake waters and wore out their legs pumping paddle boats. I enjoyed doing nothing while they played. By late afternoon the sky began to darken; storm clouds began to appear above the sweet gum and bald cypress trees along the northern shore of the lake.

Grace, Simon, and Nick reluctantly helped to pack up pic-nic paraphernalia and swim gear. We hiked quickly back to our campsite. Fellow campers were packing up tents and stowing belongings. They warned us that the weather forecast was for severe weather before dark. Not wanting to sleep in the camper during a storm this far from civilization, I refused to listen to the kids' protests and insisted that we pack up, too.

As the sky darkened we drove about 20 miles to Mt. Pleasant, leaving the storm behind. I considered staying in a motel, but the kids insisted that camping in the rain would be exciting. As yet no rain had fallen, so I agreed to compromise by getting a campsite at a KOA on the outskirts of town.

Darkness arrived with gusts of strong wind but no rain. The cool dampness felt good after a hot day, but a greenish tinge to the evening sky worried me. We set the camper up and ate sand-wiches inside as a light drizzle began to fall.

Distant lightning followed by rumbles of thunder marched closer on the wind. The teens tried to laugh at the flapping canvas and swaying camper. Branches snapped; the canvas popped in the wind. Suddenly the roof was pelted with heavy rain and hail.

Enough of this excitement! We shrugged on ponchos. Simon swung Nick onto his back. Grace and I grabbed towels and a flashlight and waded to the van. I wanted a much stronger shelter. Fortunately the restrooms were on higher ground and were built of cement blocks. I insisted that we all go into the ladies' room so we would be together. So, from the van into the howling, slashing rain we ran.

Pushing into the restroom, we dried off. The kids began joking as the thunder and lightning intensified. A middle-aged man, his wife, and their small fuzzy dog joined us. He said that the lower section of the campground was now under water and that the manager was trying to pull large campers to higher ground. Would our camper wash away?

For several hours the sink counters provided our only place to sit, since the floor was flooded. Restlessly we waited out the storm. At last the thunder and lightning seemed to dissipate slightly. Everyone wanted to go check on the camper. Not wanting us to separate, we all dashed through the pouring rain to the van.

Parts of the roadway were under several inches of water, but we were able to park near our campsite. Grace and Nick stayed in the van, while Simon and I waded through knee-deep water to find water rushing under the camper. Fortunately water had not yet gotten on the floor. We climbed inside to check for leaks and to gather more towels and dry clothing.

Once back in the van, I drove through rising water to park in front of the restrooms. Dreading the drenching we would receive running back inside, we agreed to try and sleep huddled up in the van. Through the steamed-up windows, we saw wind-whipped branches through flashes of lightning. Hail pelted the roof. Repeated crashes of thunder shook us out of dozing.

Dawn crept around the security lights. The rain had slackened to a drizzle, so we drove on flooded pavement as far as we dared. Water lapped at the underside of the camper, so we all waded in to push and pull it clear of the floodwater and onto the roadway. Shaking the canvas to pop off as much water as possible, we lowered the roof and hitched up. A few RVs had been driven or pulled to higher ground, but several others were in deep water.

On the way into town the kids commented that no lights were on and that the signal lights were out. Fortunately for my hungry crew after their long night's ordeal, Nick spotted the golden arches of a McDonalds. A teenaged girl welcomed us at the drive-through window. She chattered nervously. The restaurant had just gotten electricity back on, so our order would take a while. A tornado had struck several businesses in town and had taken the roof off of the motel were I had wanted to stay.

California or Bust

The scare of our first outing faded into jokes, as we planned our first major trip: Houston to Fresno, California. Grace wanted desperately to reconnect with long-lost relatives in California. Simon preferred the trip to alternative arrangements. Nick was always happy to travel.

Our family had increased by the adoption of Darrell, age four. Legally blind, Darrell could see well enough to be mobile. He was developmentally delayed, didn't talk, and was not potty trained. Diapers. Yuck. His seizures were under medical control. Although he often had temper tantrums, he loved to ride and to eat. The other kids were willing helpers who understood his limitations, so planning began.

Packing for five people for two weeks was a challenge. Food staples, supplies, utensils, charcoal, and tools went under the camper's benches. Clothes were packed in duffel bags and stored on the floor under the back platform. The grill, water jugs, and sleeping bags were stuffed in the aisle. An ice box cooler and a picnic box with a day's supply of goodies were closest to the door and could be reached without raising the camper roof. Everyone had a personal bag or backpack in the back of the van.

Our first major stop was Big Bend National Park, one of my favorite places since a trip many years ago. I wanted my East Texans to experience the real West, with desert, mountains, cactus, and the Rio Grande. Turning due south from Marathon, I couldn't interest them in any more deserts, mountains, or cactus. So while they slept, I recalled my first experience with the country described as the place where God dumped all the leftover rocks after He created Texas.

I'm including that first-experience story even though I wasn't single on the trip. My then-husband, Tom, and my two oldest daughters, then ages 8 and 10, and I made the trip in the early 1970's in an old van. That trip began on Christmas Day with two canoes strapped on the roof, two bikes mounted on the front of the van, and two bikes on a rear carrier. As if we weren't crowded enough, we took along a Siberian husky and a Samoyed.

As we turned south out of Marathon, the sun began to slide behind distant mountain ranges. In order to see the approach to Big Bend, we pulled off the road at a rest area for the night.

As the sun began to lighten the eastern mountain range, we followed the narrow ribbon road, swooping down into draws with 6- to 7-foot flood gauges. Desert hills sparsely covered with creosote bush, cactus, and dry prickly desert plants receded toward the distant mountain ranges on either side. The remains of an occasional barbed-wire fence trapped tumble weeds. We saw no electric poles, homes, or other vehicles in any directions. Long-eared jack rabbits and a few mule-deer ventured into sight. A couple of vultures and high-soaring hawks kept us company for the long, 60-mile drive.

Far to the south, the parallel mountain ranges seemed to break and reassemble and then to converge. Rounding the base of a mountainous outcrop, the road began to climb into Panther

Junction. Here was a small ranger station, where visitors got permits to travel further into the wilderness.

This was the year of the first, great gasoline shortage, but we had been determined to make the trip anyway. We were advised that the primitive sites along the lower river road were closed because of the gas shortage. However, we could use a site down one of the gravel roads that ended on the Rio Grande; gas was available at Rio Grande City. Our site was perfect. Our nearest neighbors were camped quite a distance away; they soon packed up and left. Nothing marked the sites except trash barrels scattered on this prairie, high above the Rio Grande.

Tom, Colleen, the dogs and I hiked up the nearest mountainside, leaving Cheri to putter around the van. We could see her clearly as we climbed, so we were confident she would not wander off. Then we noticed an animal sniffing around one of the distant trash barrels. Cheri became aware of the large dog and started toward it. We watched in horror as we realized it was no dog but a large coyote.

Realizing her mistake, Cheri began to back off and then turned to return to the van. We breathed that sigh of relief of good parents whose child passes the test; we began to scramble down off the mountain. Now she would close the doors and roll up the windows, we thought.

But not my daughter. She sat in the driver's seat as the coyote approached the van and began to sniff it over. Before we reached the plateau to run to her rescue, she was throwing dog food out the door to get the coyote to come closer.

Cheri called to us as we ran. "Did you see that? I almost got him in the van!" she yelled exultantly. We never let Cheri get out of reach again, much less out of sight.

We joined another family on an overnight canoe trip through Boquillos canyon. The men registered our plan with the Ranger and checked out the weather forecast. They did a car shuffle and dropped a car off at our take-out point so we would have a way back.

Cheri and I shared one canoe, Tom and Colleen the other. We launched on the Rio Grande near the small village ranger station. Here the river cut through a plain bordered by low, rolling hills and river cane. The shallow river rippled and splashed over fallen rock. Suddenly the current picked up speed; we were thrown to the base of a low overhang. Rapids began to form to test our skills.

Then came an abrupt left hook in the river channel; we faced the awesome "V" entrance to Boquillos canyon. Vertical cliffs now extended towards the heavens, boxing us in on the river. Many miles of shallow rapids flowing north, with vertical walls on either side; desert vegetation isolated us from civilization. The glaring sun began to diminish as it passed overhead and to the West. A cluster of boulders provided a dry docking for a lunch break.

Late in the afternoon a sandbar welcomed us. We hoisted the canoes high up on the sloping footing of the mountain and pitched tents on the most level spots we could find. Fortunately the temperature appeared to be too cold for rattlesnakes to be out at night. Rain was not in the forecast, but we had been warned to camp well above possible unexpected high water.

My girls feared the isolation and the wilderness. I struggled to suppress my own apprehensions and pointed out bird calls, coyote howls, and the millions of stars that glittered overhead on this cold, clear night. I reassured myself that the Rangers knew where we were and that they would look for us if we faced true danger.

Morning light was deceiving. In the shadowy bottom of this deep canyon, the sun's light was weak until almost noon, and then with the sun directly overhead, it became quite hot. Our course continued on a northward flow of ripples and small rapids.

Canyon walls began to slowly recede among jumbles of boulders and silt that had eroded over the centuries from the Sierra del Carmon mountain range.

A small, wood-planked pier jutted from the left bank—the first sign of human inhabitance we had seen in two days. The men walked up a dirt track while we waited with our canoes and gear, hoping that this was the ranch were they had left a car for our return. Again I struggled with thoughts of being stranded. The murmur of a car engine brought welcome relief.

Back in our campsite, we decided to relocate. On the way out of this desolate area, the van's transmission went out. We could not go forward in any gear. We backed off the gravel road to avoid blocking it; we waited. Since we had not seen any other travelers or occupied campsites, waiting for help could be indefinite.

All four of us mounted our bikes and carried empty, gallon milk jugs to get water. The two dogs followed us as we rode those bikes up and down hills for five miles to the Park Ranger station at Rio Grande Village.

Here we reported our mechanical problems and filled up on water. It was now late Friday afternoon. The ranger gave us permission to camp where we were stranded and promised to check on us. The following afternoon we rode again for water, this time leaving the dogs with their sore feet in the van. On Sunday afternoon a Ranger arrived with the Parks Department tow truck and towed our loaded van to Panther Junction. We were allowed to sleep in the van in the parking lot next to the "No overnight parking" sign.

On Monday arrangements were made with the closest transmission repair shop to send a tow truck. That evening we were towed 450 miles to Odessa. Our van was dropped off in the shop's parking lot. This was to be our next campsite. That night it was so cold that all four of us, fully dressed, slept close together in the back of the van under all the sleeping bags, with both dogs on top for warmth.

The weather was so cold that my contact lenses froze in their case of solution and had to be thawed over a steaming coffee pot heated on a Coleman stove. Our jugs of water had a thick layer of ice. Snow had fallen during the night. It was New Year's Day; the shop, as well as most of the town, was closed. As anxious as we were to get the van repaired, we took a walking tour and patiently waited.

FOUR

Westward Ho

On that first trip to Big Bend, my daughters discovered a huge sand slide near the mouth of the Boquillos Canyon. I was certain that my new family would enjoy the sand slide as much as we had then. On this latest trip we settled the camper into a campsite in Rio Grande Village campground and then drove to the parking lot at the base of the Rio Grande overlook.

By holding someone's hand and listening to "step up" or "step down" as we hiked, Darrell was able to make the long climb up a steep trail to the overlook. After a brief stop at the overlook, we turned to descend single file into a narrow tunnel in a thicket of river cane.

Huge spires of canes with narrow sharp-edged leaves towered over us blocking out the sun. Rustling and rattling of the poles in the breeze was spooky. The cane brake grew so thick that a person could not break through them and had to stay on the winding trail.

Eventually the canes began to thin out. A mountainside of boulders was glimpsed through the tops of the canes. Grace, behind me, screamed! We all stopped and quickly returned to her. She had attempted to catch her balance on a boulder protruding through the cane and had almost put her hand down on a snake sunning itself. The frightened snake slithered away. Simon and Nick wanted to hunt it down and catch it. I vetoed.

Remember, I cautioned them, take only pictures; leave only footprints!

The murmur of water rushing over stones reached us before we saw the river bank. Hearing the water, Darrell tried to pull me into the Rio Grande. If he had gotten his way, he would have rushed right in. I lured him away over a ridge of stones to play in the sand while the rest of the kids skipped water-tumbled stones on the cold shallow river.

The open "V" of Boquillos Canyon beckoned the kids to follow the river bank and explore the canyon mouth. Rounding a boulder field, I searched the mountainside for the sand slide. I saw it! A shallow cave, high up on the steep, mountain wall, had been carved by blowing sand. The resulting eroded sand cascaded down the mountain, piling deeper and deeper to form a steep slide.

I pointed out the cave to the kids. Seeing people the size of ants in the mouth of the cave, my daredevils ran around boulders to the base of the slide and started to climb. On hands and knees they climbed the shifting sand and slid back down. They discarded their shoes and threw them down to me.

Over and over they climbed and slid backward until someone noticed that they could get better footing if they climbed near a rocky outcropping along the edge of the sand. Darrell and I stayed behind and played in the sand at the base of the slide.

Reaching the top, my kids entered the shallow cave to look around. I watched as they pushed each other, laughing, on the brink of the sand lip until they all had fallen in the sand. One by one they slid on the seat of their pants to the bottom. They raced each other back to the top, whooping and yelling. I marveled how easily teenagers could revert to kids if the circumstances encouraged their sense of freedom.

Tiring of the sand in our clothing and getting hungry, we hiked past the slide and into the "V" of the canyon between the rushing river and the steep mountainsides until we reached the end of the accessible trail. Shear mountain cliffs and huge boulders blocked our access to the canyon. Only an occasional canoe or Mexican rancher on horseback riding in the river could explore farther.

I planned to take my kids on a trail ride from the Chisos Basin high in the mountains to the Window, a cleft in the high rock face that permits viewers to see many miles over the western desert. On our first trip to Big Bend Country, we had taken my older girls on this beautiful trail ride. I hoped I could experience it again. I thought we might have a problem getting permission for Darrell to ride double with me, but our actual disappointment occurred because a weight limit existed for the horses. No one over 200 pounds could ride; one of my teens topped 200. I couldn't go and leave one, so we canceled. We were all very disappointed. The kids couldn't understand that at that high altitude—6,000 feet—weight was a safety issue for the horses.

After breaking camp we retraced our route north to Marathon and then continued westward, settling into a routine of teens squabbling about everything and Nick trying to avoid helping out. Darrell enjoyed riding and was content as long as he didn't get hungry. New Mexico and Arizona were boring to the teens. Turning north out of Phoenix, Arizona, we entered Joshua Tree National Park. The temperature was over 100 degrees; the sun blazed in a clear, cloudless sky. We remarked on the desert plants, the heat waves on the highway, lack of traffic, no signs of humanity. To break the boredom and the squabbling, I suggested a "what-if?" game. What if we had a flat tire? What should we do?

Simon remembered that we had several gallon milk jugs that they had reluctantly filled with water. Grace recalled that some cacti could be skinned and sucked for water. They both agreed it would be too hot to stay in the van, even with the doors and windows open. They decided that they would stretch a tarp out from the side of the trailer for shade. And we would pray for someone to pass by.

Fortunately our game was only a game. Or so we thought. Around 4 p.m., I pulled into a service station in Needles, on the Arizona/California border, for gas. The attendant called me over and showed me a bulging, cracked tire that had to be replaced.

While we sat on the curb in the shade, we thanked God that our game had not been for real. A thermometer, hanging on the front of the station in the shade, read 120 degrees.

Our visit to California included tracking down Grace's relatives in the Fresno area, exploring the giant redwood trees, and, at the teens' insistence, a visit to the beach in Los Angles. I fought the congested freeway traffic that fortunately was slow enough so I could follow the highway markers. The beach we located was windy and cold. Our visit was at mid-week, so we saw few surfers and not much surf. I kept Darrell back in the sand dunes to play and to keep him out of the frigid water, while the older kids braved the clear, gray, icy water. We stayed long enough to say, "Been there, done that."

None of us was interested in seeing Hollywood, so we located a KOA near the beach. It was the most expensive campground I had stayed in and was extremely crowded for mid-week. I squeezed in between a bus-sized motor home and a very large travel trailer. We looked like the poor relations. We had barely enough room to open the doors and pull out the beds. Fires were not allowed, so we made supper of sandwiches.

The teens headed to find the recreation room while I put Darrell to bed and read to Nick. Later, Grace came back and said that they were going to play pool for a while longer with some teens they had met. I warned her that it was getting late and I couldn't leave the little ones to hunt for them, so they could only stay out for another hour. Several hours later, I was panicked. Then she returned without Simon and said she thought he had returned before her. She offered to go look for him. I tried to hide my fears, but it was well past quiet hour. I let her know I had been worrying. With the little ones asleep, I let her go look for Simon.

Midnight arrived and passed. Neither one had returned. By now I was less worried and more angry. The campground was supposed to have security, but I didn't see anyone pass by who looked like security personnel. I was certain that the game room had been closed for hours. Where were they?

I feared leaving the little ones for long, but I walked back and forth between the camper, the closed game room, and the restrooms in the cold night air, past dark campers parked in the shadows. I finally gave up, returned one last time to the camper, and dozed off.

Sometime during the early hours, those two crept back in and were sound asleep when Darrell woke me at dawn. I made them both get up to help break camp. They offered no explanations except that they were visiting with kids at another site and lost track of time. I was furious. And relieved. As soon as we were on the highway, they feel asleep.

Miles down the road when they got into another argument, Grace ratted on Simon. According to her, he had gotten beer from the kids at the game room and was drunk. She had stayed with him to keep him out of trouble. He denied it, of course, and said that it was she who was drunk. I reasoned that they were both guilty and were fortunate to have found their way back to the camper rather than jail.

We returned to Texas by the South Rim of the Grand Canyon. I had not been there since I was on that camping trip when I was very young. The vistas were absolutely majestic. This awesome monument to God's handiwork would continue to stagger me years later. Watching people begin to descend the Bright Angel trail, I ached to attempt a trip to the bottom of the canyon but not with two small children. I preferred to take a mule ride, not to hike. Someday.

That night, camping in a state park south of the Grand Canyon, we could see snow on the distant mountain tops. The temperature was falling. Fortunately sleeping bags had been crammed into storage; now we pulled them out. This is June? That night the temperature fell below freezing. By morning the kids could claim to have seen a few snowflakes.

Near the Texas border, Grace and Simon began another miles-long, verbal fight. She threatened to deck him. He challenged her to a fight. She was several inches taller and much heavier than he, but he had a temper of his own. Most of the time he was a gentleman and ignored her taunting. This time it looked like blows.

I pulled over on the shoulder of the hot, deserted highway and told them both to get out. They did. She yelled that he talked dirty and swung at him. He ducked. His defensive punch knocked her back. I got out, slowly, and went around the van. Their fistfight was evenly matched and was mostly bluff. By the time I told them to break it up, they were both ready to back off. Grace insisted that she would walk home. She trudged off down the road in the noonday sun. I took a break and followed. It wasn't long before she decided that she would let us pick her up and would permit us to give her a ride to Houston.

FIVE

Discovering Dinosaurs

By 1988, my family had changed again. Grace and Simon were no longer at home. Darrell was essentially still functioning as he did at three years old—still not potty-trained. Nick, a fun-loving 10-year-old, now had six adopted siblings. My children's ages ranged from six to 13. They had all been taken on short camping trips and all, except Darrell, participated in Scouting.

"Grandma's on the phone!" yelled Joanna.

I spoke with my mother briefly and took the TV remote control from protesting Joe.

"Your grandmother said that my cousin, David, is going to be on PBS tonight". I switched channels just in time to catch an introduction to Dr. David Weishampel, paleontologist. "Everybody, quiet. Sit down and watch."

Groans, accompanied by "Do we have to?" "I bet it's educational. " "No fun!"

Cousin Dave presented his findings of maisasaur dinosaur eggs in Montana and then presented his theory that the parasorolophos dinosaur could make trumpeting noises by blowing air though the bony horn on its head, like an elephant trumpeting through its trunk.

My kids were fascinated. Even though the program was educational, they were excited that they had a famous cousin involved with their favorite creatures.

From the TV station we ordered a tape of the program to show at their schools. The kids wrote letters to Doctor Dave and included drawings of their favorite dinosaurs. Nick was so enthusiastic that for his science-fair project, he built a replica of David's dino horn, based on the TV program. The five-foot-long noisemaker drove the rest of us crazy.

Months later, we received a reply from Dave, whom I'd never met, and a casual invitation to visit him, his wife, and two daughters, someday, on their summer dig in Montana. Always eager to travel, I thought, "Why not?" "Why not take eight kids in a pop-up camper from Houston, Texas to Montana?"

I should have heeded Robert Benchley, who said, "In America there are two classes of travel—first class and with children."[1]

We had only a few obstacles to overcome, like the cost of food and gas and bribes to behave, sleeping arrangements, travel route, and itinerary. And whether I could tolerate my kids non-stop, in a 13-passenger van for three weeks without TV. I was reminded that mothers don't keep bankers' hours; they're open 24 hours a day. Without pay. Was I setting myself up for a nervous breakdown?

Gullible and optimistic, I began planning by getting the kids interested. Dinosaur hunting excited them all, but the idea of sharing a van seat and tent space with siblings was another story.

Determination Reigns

The PBS program had aired on TV in December. By the next December, I was determined to take my kids dinosaur hunting in every place we could find from Texas to Montana. All the kids had that innate interest in dinos and secretly wanted to discover a skeleton, or better yet, find a "real" one. My kids had mixed feelings about traveling so far from home. All of them had histories of insecurity with their birthfamilies; the idea of being away from their new home was unsettling.

My favorite babysitter, Teresa (the only one willing to return to face my gang), wanted to be a paleontologist. She became more excited about our proposed trip than did her charges, so I invited her along. She would help referee the kids. I would provide her meals, and of course, transportation and lodging in the camper. She would take spending money. As our plans materialized, her enthusiasm infected the rest of the gang.

Early in the spring, I wrote to David to verify our invitation. We read his return letter with apprehension. His grant for the 1990 season had not yet been approved.

But on May 10, we received another letter. Things were then official! The National Science Foundation had decided to smile on him for another couple of years. He would be headed out to the field once again. David added that he would be glad to have me and all the younger Weishampels out at his camp for a couple of days. I noted a little concern for my troops and assured him that we wouldn't overstay our welcome because, as we on the Gulf Coast say, fish and guests begin to stink after three days.

Planning in earnest, I took apart an old U.S. atlas and began to highlight places of interest, especially anything having to do with dinosaurs. We checked out library books and noted dinosaur parks on our maps. Yellowstone National Park! I shivered. Here was a place I had dreamed of visiting. We would see Old Faithful! I worked out a circular route that included nine states and appeared to be a more than 3,000-mile round trip. Highlighting the proposed route on a full U.S. map made the trip become more real.

To involve the kids, I made copies of the map of each state that we would pass through and put them in a pocket folder with a colored marker, notebook paper, and pencils. I hoped that each one would trace our route as we traveled and would keep a journal, or at least make a few drawings and collect some postcards and brochures. The kids could share a few inexpensive cameras.

I wrote to Dave again to verify that his invitation was genuine. His return letter invited us to "visit when you can", but I sensed that he doubted we'd take him up on it.

Little did he know of my determination to do the seemingly impossible—take eight kids on a 3,000-mile trip in three weeks.

Dave sent vague directions and a hand-drawn map to his dig site near Browning, Montana, in the far northwestern part of the state, near Glacier National Park. My excitement grew.

Our maps began to take shape. We had our destination, places to visit, and a time frame. We'd leave as soon as school was out in June. The kids still had mixed feelings about being away from home. Teresa and I debated whether they could get along with each other in a 13-passenger van for that long.

In April the kids and I moved the pop-up camper into the shade of huge oak trees, where we popped the tent up, pulled out the beds, and began work on it. The musty, dusty smell was awful. Kids cleaned out the cubbyholes, cleaned the mattresses, and swept down the netting and floor. I stitched up some split seams in the canvas.

"We're not using that thing!" We voted to leave the port-a-potty home and make do with rest stops.

Darrell's tantrums had worsened as he grew. His mental development had not increased with his age. He was now seven; behaviorally and developmentally he was still about 24 months. He had outgrown the largest stroller available and was so uncooperative walking that I had stopped taking him out in public. After a particularly violent episode in the doctor's office, his doctor recommended a wheelchair with a harness to hold him in. This arrangement was a godsend. Now it was possible to control him so he could not grab unsuspecting people and pull their clothes, or pull out of our grasp to throw himself on the floor.

Darrell was a handsome boy who did not look handicapped. To strangers he just acted like a "brat." But in his wheelchair, others accepted Darrell's strange behavior and gave him the space he needed.

Darrell's doctor put him on new medication for seizures that made him less active than usual. This was a blessing, because he was not as irritable and was much more cooperative. We all agreed that he would be manageable. No one considered trying to find a temporary residence for Darrell and taking the trip without him.

The wheelchair would make taking Darrell on the trip more feasible, if I could figure out how to carry it. Even though it folded, it was too bulky to fit in the rear of the van with all the other stuff. I finally got an inspiration and talked to my neighbor. Mr. Hart, a retired gentleman, was a welder. From a bed frame we designed a metal rack to fit on top of the camper. Mr. Hart welded large eyebolts to the front corners of the camper roof. A welding rod was inserted through the eyebolts; the metal frame was welded to the rod so that the rod acted as a hinge. The frame could be pivoted up off the roof to form a lid. The tallest kids helped lay a folded tarp on the roof. The wheelchair, and bulky luggage fit inside the tarp and were held in place by the frame and a lot of rope.

My yellow pad now had many lists of supplies, menus, groceries, endless stuff for kids, sleeping bags, and duffels for clothes (one large and one small per kid. The large one was to be packed in the camper. The small one had to hold everything the kid wanted in the van. If something didn't fit, it got left home or had to be packed in the large bag). Also in the van were a grill, sack of charcoal, cooler, car tools, first-aid kit, picnic box, water jugs, radio headsets, snacks, and a surprise box.

The surprise box was a stroke of genius. I collected a large number of inexpensive kids things: playing cards, a jump rope, colored pencils, games, crossword-puzzle books, small cars, balloons, and trinkets of all kinds, but no gum or candy. Each item was wrapped in the newspaper comic pages and stuffed in a box.

Each day as we traveled, I would keep track of behavior by the use of "black marks" in a small notebook. At the end of the day, the kid with the fewest marks would get to choose a wrapped surprise. The rules were that the winner did not have to share his or her prize.

The next day the winner could choose a previously won prize or draw from the box. If an already opened prize was chosen, then the person who had it got to pick another one as a replacement. This way favorite items would be shared.

I devised another "rule" to avoid fights over seating. At each stop the navigator—front passenger-seat driver—would be changed in the order of descending age. That way everyone would have a turn in the front and would get separated from the others. If someone wanted to pass up his turn, he or she could, but that child had to wait a full cycle for a next turn on the front seat. Three of my sons were very clannish and would probably give in to the oldest boy, no matter what he wanted, but I didn't care who sat up front with me as long as each one had a turn who wanted one and I could separate antagonists.

Since my kids were not the most cooperative and were sneaky, I bought a large, clip-on, rear-view mirror. It increased the view of what I could see going on behind my back.

I figured that sleeping arrangements for 10 when the camper only slept six very friendly people could be solved by taking two tents.

Then, in May, as our plans began to finalize, my family increased with the addition of Christopher, my two-month-old grandson. Diapers, wipes, clothes, powdered formula, and bottled water were added to the supply lists.

Chris was a happy, healthy baby that the older girls adored. I knew he would have plenty of babysitters, but I was concerned about carrying him on hikes. To add a stroller to our overflowing rooftop carrier didn't seem to be the best idea. Then, at Goodwill I found an aluminum and canvas baby backpack. But Chris was too small to sit up in it; his head did not peek over the top. Another stroke of genius—I made a liner for the backpack from a thin sheet of foam robber, folded in half, and cut out in the shape of a large disposable diaper. I covered it with washable fabric. With the liner in the backpack, Chris was sandwiched in so that he was held upright. His head was supported; he could see out. He was a large taco! The girls vied over who would get to carry him.

Another concern I had about traveling with a baby was the threat of mosquitoes. The local druggist did not recommend any of the repellents for a baby this young. Checking with Avon Products, I was assured that its popular product, Skin So Soft, was safe for use on a baby. It worked for him and the others.

[1]John Bartlett, *Familiar Quotations* (Boston, New York, London: Little, Brown & Son), 675.

SIX

On the Road to Dino Discovery

At last we were on the road. The oldest child was navigator; baby Chris was in a carseat with Cora as his attendant; and Teresa was in the center of the back seat, separating potential squabblers. Behind the back seat, a large assortment of necessities were packed. Following behind came our camper, stuffed to capacity with the wheelchair on the roof.

We made a lunch stop near Brenham. And got off to a bad start. I got stung by a wasp, Roy started running a fever, and both Nick and Joe got a spanking for fighting.

Late on our first afternoon, we arrived at Dinosaur Valley State Park in Glen Rose, Texas. We set up the camper with a minimum amount of bickering, changed into swimwear, and hiked off to explore the Paluxy River.

The western edge of the parking lot dropped off an embankment that led to the river. Not following the marked trail, my boys scrambled down the bluff. We girls, Darrell, and the baby cautiously followed the marked trail down log-reinforced steps to the river bank.

The boys threw their shoes off and were splashing in the cold water. Although shallow, the water rushed over small boulders, causing strong currents and deeper pools. We settled Darrell in a pool to splash. I stayed behind with the baby while the others picked their way across the stones and shallow water to the far side of the river.

There they discovered a roped-off area that protected fossil dinosaur tracks in what had once been the soft sediment of the river. We were on the right track to discover all we could about dinosaurs.

On the hike back to the campground, Joe yelled and point-ed above the tops of distant oak trees. Poking above the top most branches was what appeared to be the head of a long neck dinosaur! The four boys took off running through the brush and scrub oaks, disregarding the trails. We yelled at them to wait for us, but, of course, they didn't. So Teresa and the girls took off after them while I brought up the rear with the baby and Darrell.

There they were—two huge dinosaurs behind a chain-link fence. They were Fiberglass models that had been relocated here from the New York World's Fair. One was a T-Rex with a wide-open mouth full of teeth. The other was an Apatasaurus. The long neck's tiny head was what Joe had seen over the trees. The boys were trying to climb the fence to get a closer look when I arrived to warn them to get down. Disappointed that the dinosaurs were only fakes, they reluctantly agreed to return to camp and help get dinner ready. Cora won the first day's prize.

Raccoons thrashing the trash cans and attempting to get into our supplies kept us all awake. What a racket! After a late breakfast of breakfast burritos—sausage and eggs scrambled together and served wrapped in tortillas—we packed the camper and headed back to the main highway. A large sign, "Creation Science Museum", near a bend in the Paluxy River intrigued me. Curious, I turned in through the gate and followed a dirt road to a small building.

A tiny museum was begun in the mid-80's after a group of Christians began to study dinosaur and human footprints in the same strata of the Paluxy River. These tracks had originally been found more than 50 years ago on several different sites. In one location the tracks continued beneath a cliff, under 20 feet of overburden. News reporters had been witnesses as a backhoe excavated the area, exposing footprints that could not have been faked. One print seemed to be of a huge, three-toed dinosaur with a human print superimposed on it. It seemed similar to an elephant leaving a print in the mud. Before it dried, a human stepped in it. Then the print was rapidly filled with flowing sediment and preserved under water pressure as a fossil imprint. Could it be that dinosaurs and humans lived at the same time?

The Bible states that God created animals and then humans on the same day, but in public school, I had been taught that millions of years were required for creatures to evolve. Therefore, dinosaurs had to have lived and become extinct before humans evolved from apes. In Sunday school my kids and I had learned about Creation in the Book of Genesis, but no one had attempted to address the conflict. Our visit to the small museum raised many questions I could not answer.

As we headed north on Interstate 35, the evolution-Creation conflict nagged at me. My sons settled into bickering with the girls, while everyone complained about the boring scenery, boring trip, boring seatmates. Finally they dozed; I contemplated dinosaurs. Public school and college had indoctrinated me to a millions-of-years-old earth, with dinosaurs becoming extinct millions of years before apes evolved into humans. My Bible taught that humans and animals were created, but I had never learned that it mentioned dinosaurs. Maybe each day of Creation was as a thousand years; then dinosaurs could have been created and died out before humans were created.

Reaching Kansas we turned west toward Dodge City and Colorado. What is that horrible smell? Rude comments about seatmates and opening the windows didn't help. Any possible guilty parties were exonerated as stockyards appeared over the flat horizon. Stockyards packed full of cattle edged both sides of the highway and stretched endlessly in all directions. For miles and miles, the kids complained about "cow perfume."

Our itinerary included Royal Gorge and a tram ride to the bottom of the gorge, then the Grand Tetons and Yellowstone. Old Faithful, the paint pots burping, a hailstorm, moose, and bears kept the kids' interest. What do they remember most? The outhouse.

Somewhere on the vast plains of Wyoming we turned off the highway, following a sign for a campground. The narrow, paved road passed over gently rolling prairie seemingly to lead to nowhere.

The pavement deteriorated into dirt tracks, crossed over a bridge at the lower end of a small lake in the hollow of a fringe of grass-covered hills. Past the bridge the track shifted to native gravel.

As the sun was setting, we spotted another sign. We crossed the grassy plain to an area marked "camping". Campsites were unmarked, so we stopped near a cement-block restroom, the only building on the prairie. Out they all scrambled. The girls' side of the restroom was primitive but served the basic needs. I heard a yell from the boys' side. Then another yell. Approaching the door, I called, "Now what?", fearing they had caught a snake.

Joe, Nick, and Roy answered simultaneously from inside, "We're locked in! We can't get out! The door's stuck!"

Hearing the noise, the girls had followed me around to the boys' door. "Leave them in there!" they laughed.

I tried the door. Stuck. Jammed. "Unlock it, you guys."

"We tried! It won't work. The lock's broke."

I jiggled the knob. The girls kicked the door, laughing. The boys inside rammed it with their puny shoulders.

"Can you take the hinges apart?" I suggested.

"No! Get us out of here!"

I sent Joanna to tell Phillip to get a crowbar and tool box from the van. I wasn't sure what I was going to do, but at least I seemed to be in control. We went around to the back of the building. A small window was high up on the wall. I saw hands. Joe, standing on the toilet, waved to us. A quick survey of the treeless, deserted campground revealed no other humans. What to do? Leave Phillip here and take the others with me back to the highway? Then what? Where was a town? The sun was sinking rapidly.

50

Phillip brought the crowbar and tools and attacked the door lock with the bar. The metal door didn't give. He yelled back and forth to his "wimpy" younger brothers, then went around back and stared at the small window.

"Boost me up there."

"What for?" I asked

Macho man said, "I'll get them out."

I gave him a leg up. He grabbed the window ledge and pulled himself over it. The girls whooped louder, seeing his front half disappear into the window and his back-side hanging outside. "A mugwump!" they yelled. (Definition: A "mugwump" is a bird on a wire with his mug on one side and his "wump" on the other.)

"Phillip. Don't you dare go in there!" I yelled as the other boys pulled him in, headfirst. Now all four were locked in the outhouse.

"I know what I'm doing," he boasted.

Joe's head and shoulders appeared in the window. He was being pushed through by the others. We caught him as he slid headfirst down the wall. One out. Three to go. Next appeared Nick. Then Roy, the smallest, sliding down the wall headfirst into the girls' helpful hands. Phillip was left. Our strong, silent hero was left. The girls jumped up and down, calling out suggestions. He refused to answer my calls. At last we saw his hands over the window ledge. And his head appeared. He pulled himself up and across the ledge. The window was too narrow for him to turn around and descend feet first, so he reluctantly allowed me to catch him as he slid headfirst toward the ground.

The boys pounded him on the back and whooped congratulations.

The girls bombarded him with questions, "How did you do it?"

"Easy. I just stood on the toilet and pushed them out."

SEVEN

Dave's Dino Digs

After 10 grueling, exasperating, exciting days on the road, we pulled out the map to Cousin Dave's dig, Camp-No-Slack. Out of Browning, Montana, we drove over gravel roads through Indian lands past a small ranch house and down a sloped track that disappeared into the woods. Teepees! Through the trees, the kids spotted several Indian teepees. We had arrived. The camp was empty. No one was around. Figuring that they were all at the dig site, we began to explore.

As we followed the trail near a river bank, Teresa turned and faced us all. "I've had it with all of you!" she announced.

Teresa was my peacemaker. While I drove, she arbitrated. She willingly helped change the baby and tended to Darrell, but the older kids' constant bickering had worn her down. She had enough extra money to buy a plane ticket home and was ready to call it quits. Phillip, Joanna, and Christina each started blaming each other. The younger kids begged her not to leave them. I needed her help and was willing to beg on bended knees for her to reconsider. Instead I backed her up, telling the whole gang that I was so disgusted with their behavior that I was tempted to leave them all here in the middle of a deserted Indian camp and go back with Teresa.

After much stomping and accusing, macho Phillip relented and stated that he would "lay off" Joanna if she quit picking fights with Christina. Christina and Joanna agreed on a truce. The younger two boys also agreed to try a truce and quit ganging up on Nick. Cora, as usual, was congenial and neutral.

Darrell and baby Chris were as happy as always as long as they weren't hungry. Much to my relief, Teresa decided to try to stick it out for a while longer. She would tolerate them just for the experience of working on the dig with real paleontologists. I herded my reformed outlaws back towards the main camp just as Dave, his wife Judy, their two young daughters and several college students drove up in a convoy of dusty pickup trucks.

Dave welcomed us. Yes, he had gotten my letter, but I could tell he didn't expect us to show up. He wasn't sure what to think of my crew. Introductions were made around. One of the students gave us a tour of the outhouse. A small authentic, well-worn teepee, set off by itself, housed a deep hole, a dirt pile, a shovel, a bag of lime, and a coffee can.

Family and scholars had hand dug the pit latrine, equipped it with a hitching rail to sit on, and a toilet tissue roll propped on a forked stick.

After use, a can full of lime was to be tossed in, followed by a shovel full of dirt. This convenience had a wrap-around door fly and sported a bandanna that flew from a stick at appropriate times to signal occupancy.

The kids and Teresa agreed, for once, that this experience was worth their good behavior.

Dave and his students showed us fragments of fossilized egg shell and small bones. On the prairie they had unearthed two hadrosaur nests, complete with eggs. One of the fragmented eggs contained the skeleton of an embryo about the size of a lizard. This was the first recorded find of its kind; they were very excited about retrieving the remaining eggs and nest to submit them to CAT scans.

In another dig site, they were working on a "logjam" of mixed bones in a coulee, which, I learned, was a dry creek bed. The bones uncovered and retrieved thus far were from a variety of large dinosaurs.

We were all invited to accompany the work crew the next morning to the dig sites. So while we still had light, I took the kids to bathe in the river. All water had to be trucked in and was used for cooking and drinking only. The river was so cold that a wash-up had to do. Several students in swimsuits teased us, "Chicken tenderfoot!"

Early the next morning, we left the camper and packed into the van to follow several pick-up trucks off the dusty road and out onto the trackless prairie. Reaching the edge of a small canyon, I parked, hoisted Chris into his backpack, and we joined Dave and his students to hike to the dig site. He loaded us up with water jugs and tools to carry down the steep slope to a ledge near the bottom. Here we were taught to carefully pick dirt and rock away from the large bones they were excavating. We all took turns with dental tools and brushes in the hot sun. Teresa was ecstatic. She was able to reach her goal for making the trip. She was testing her dream of attending college to become a paleontologist. Babysitting was just a means to her goal.

I was bursting with silent questions. This site contained the jumbled bones of many different species. I was told that it appeared as if their bodies had been washed together down the canyon by a gigantic flood. Noah's Flood? In the opinion of these experts, these fossils were millions of years old. Way before Noah's time. Afraid to show my ignorance, I kept quiet.

We were hot and had little shade. The air was dusty. By mid-afternoon we were all well-educated in the process of fossil excavation. We each had turns picking at the edges of bones exposed in the rock and had the thrill of prying bone loose. We watched as fossil bones were wrapped with cloth soaked in plaster and prepared for transportation. One of the students photographed the site, while another carefully made drawings on a grid to record and firmly establish the bones' relationships and depth. When the sun passed its zenith, I returned to the van with Darrell and the baby and waited for the others. Hot and tired, my kids helped pack up the gear and climbed back to the parked vehicles. Dave wanted to visit another site before leaving the bad lands. We followed him over the rutted plains to a site where they had exposed hadrosaur nests.

The flat prairie dropped into a broad, deep depression. One nest had already been chipped and pried loose from the surrounding rock and lifted by helicopter to the flat bed of a large truck. The nest had been hauled to a museum. The remaining nest was at the bottom of the large, rocky, bowl-shaped valley. We scrambled and slid down the gravel to inspect a roughly circular, nest-shaped rock, four to five feet in diameter. Within its shallow depression were many foot-long, oval eggs. Most of the eggs were crushed, shattered, or finely cracked, but they definitely looked like eggs haphazardly arranged in a shallow nest. The students had already cleaned the area. They were now carefully prying the entire nest loose from the underlying rock so it could be coated in plaster and airlifted.

Hot, dirty, tired, but excited, my reluctant travelers were taken over by the students and were fully indoctrinated in fossil field study. They visited the lab tent to see work in progress and became friends with everyone. We must have made a good impression, because we were all invited to eat dinner with the field team. Of course we agreed and contributed to the pot luck. The college students took my kids under their wings for stories and songs around a campfire.

Several fascinating days later, as we were preparing to leave, Dave suggested we visit the Royal Tyrrell Museum of Paleontology in Drumheller, Canada. I got out my maps.

Glacier National Park was not too far out of the way to the west. We began driving west over the Going to the Sun Highway, through the mountains. Steep cliffs guarded one side of the road. Nothing but low, stone walls protected us from plunging thousands of feet off the other side. The boys exclaimed, "Cool!" The girls preferred not to look. I tried to keep my eyes on the road, willing to miss the scenery. I was conscious of the trailer swaying and scared that it would run over us on a descent or keep me from braking safely.

We reached the visitors center and parked next to plowed snow drifts. My kids had never seen snow close enough to touch. They were out of the van before I could set the parking brake. In shorts and T-shirts, they climbed on the hard-packed snow, made snow balls, and pelted each other. Soon the girls realized that they were cold, with snow in their shoes and spattered on their exposed skin. They retreated to the van for sweatshirts and jeans. My macho boys laughed at them, although shivering, and continued to play.

Teresa and I bundled Darrell and the baby snugly and insisted that the boys get jackets. We all went for a short hike. In the shadows the air was quite cold, but as we walked into the sunshine, the air temperature warmed considerably. This would take some getting used to, if a person lived here, I thought.

Not expecting to leave the United States, I had not brought any of the children's birth certificates and not thought of passports. I did have their Medicaid cards and guardianship papers for the baby. At the international border, I was asked to go inside to fill out papers while an immigration officer agreed to watch my kids in the van. All went smoothly until I returned to the van. Chaos! The kids and Teresa were hollering, "Mom! Mom !"

The officer was laughing hysterically. Joe had locked Nick's toy handcuffs to the overhead seatbelt support with Nick's wrist firmly locked in. Joe couldn't find the key. The officer tried his keys. The kids thought this was great. Just as I was warily approaching, the officer got Nick loose. He handed me the handcuffs and seemed happy to see us leave!

Once safely on the road, Teresa giggled as she told what happened while I was in the office, before the handcuff incident. An officer had stooped and looked in the window unbelievingly at all the kids and asked Teresa to whom they belonged. She answered that they were all mine. Not believing her, he asked the kids with whom they were traveling. "Mom!" they had all yelled!

Teresa laughed that he had a most puzzled look that said, "What single woman in her right mind would travel from Texas to Canada with 10 kids if they weren't hers?"

Dino Delights

We camped overnight at Dinosaur Provincial Park, a working field station with a small museum. Then on to the Tyrrell. Only open since 1985, this museum is a major research center and one of the largest paleontological museums in the world. I paired off the kids, gave each group a map of the museum, and designated a time and a meeting place.

We spent several hours in the exhibits of reconstructed dinosaur skeletons, animated models, and even a large window viewing a working lab. We hated to leave. At the appointed time I'd locate one group, insist that they stay put, go look for the others, and find that the first bunch would be gone. They took turns getting lost. Finally I bribed them. "Be outside the gift shop in exactly 30 minutes, or no souvenirs!" It worked.

Heading South back toward home, I pondered over the vast displays at Tyrrell. How could such delicate plants and fragile tiny creatures become fossilized except by being very quickly buried alive by a thick layer of sediment, then rapidly placed under the pressure of a tremendous depth of water? Noah's Flood? I pondered a fossil of a fish with its last meal, another fish, inside it.

Back through Montana, we stopped at Boseman to see the animated dinosaurs at the Museum of the Rockies. Then on toward Yellowstone National Park. This time we drove the opposite side of the figure-eight highway. This second view of Yellowstone was as fascinating as the first—especially when we ran into a bear jam . This is what the Rangers called a traffic tie-up because of all the tourists who stop their vehicles on the road to take photos of the bears.

Dinosaur National Monument near Vernal, Utah, was next on our itinerary. The roads from Vernal into Colorado were twisting and narrow, with many switchbacks and much climbing and braking. A gravel road ended at a parking lot flanked by a roofed shelter where we waited in the dry heat for a tram to take us through the mountains to the museum.

Passing through the entrance of the glass-faced quarry building, we entered a most unusual structure—a long two-storied area. The quarry-building roof enclosed the hard, sandstone mountainside which bore exposed fossils. Layers upon untold layers of fossils made up the cliffs. Before our eyes paleontologists worked on the wall of bones.

Scientists had excavated more than 2,000 fossils from the rock face since the site was discovered. A guide explained how each bone was carefully chiseled out and removed, but only if another bone was beneath it so that visitors could see bones in place. He said that this dinosaur graveyard had been formed underwater. Masses of dead dinosaurs had been washed by the current and piled on top of one another in a valley. They had been quickly covered by sediment. Later regional uplift tilted the now-hard strata into a steep angle. Then erosion began stripping away the rock to expose the bones of many different species of dinosaurs and even turtles and crocodiles.

From the upstairs balcony we watched scientists cling to the rock wall and tediously pick away at the fossils with small chisels, ice picks, and dental tools. Small chips and dust were brushed away with paintbrushes.

On the lower floor we listened intently as a guide explained the history of the museum and the significance of the find. Here, too, was a laboratory for cleaning, cataloging, and further study of specimens. The lab also made casts and molds of some of the fossils to place in exhibits.

Masses of fossils. A whole mountain of mammoth fossils, plant eaters, juveniles, and even babies, as well as turtles and crocodiles, were buried at one time.

I listened carefully as someone braver than I asked a guide what he thought caused the burial of so many animals. His answer was the movement of a tremendous volume of water that quickly drowned the animals and left a thick layer of sediment which kept the bodies from rotting before they fossilized. The guide was asked, "Noah's Flood?"

He ignored the question, but as the crowd dispersed, the guide stepped aside to reply to the brave questioner. He said that he had to give the speech and responses that he was told to give, but that he personally believed in Noah's universal flood.

With more questions than answers, we reluctantly left Dinosaur Monument and continued south. One stop was at the small museum and dinosaur gardens at Clayton, New Mexico. Here were many fine Fiberglass dinosaur models, including a pterodactyl and a huge dragonfly. Nearby Clayton Lake State Park protected some 500 tracks in thin layers of sandstone. This area was thought to once have been the shore of the Gulf of Mexico.

Our route home continued through the Texas Panhandle, with a stopover in Palo Duro Canyon, Texas's Grand Canyon, and the nearby ranching museum. Finally, three weeks later, after 3,000 miles through seven states, we all were glad to see home.

As I began to write about our great dinosaur adventure, I thought how foolish I had been not to keep a diary. Then again, I don't know when I would have had time to write while trying to keep my sanity.

When later I did write, I clearly saw that this was an experience that I'd never forget, even without notes.

Five years later, the *Houston Chronicle* Travel Section advertised a challenging contest. Entrants were to propose a three-day, two-night, fantasy vacation with a firm, $350 budget. My entry, based in part on our dino discovery trip, was chosen over 75 other entries and was published in the paper.

Following is my winning entry:

"$350 and a three day escape ALONE, away from my six kids, is my fantasy. However, after bribing a babysitter, I wouldn't have any cash left for Motel 6 and a burger, so my realistic getaway includes fun for all: single mom and kids, ages 5 to 18.

"On Thursday night we make TrailMix, freeze lemonade, and pack the van with two small tents, charcoal, picnic box with assorted kitchen stuff, a large mesh bag full of sheets and beach towels, fishing poles, football, Frisbee, assorted radios and electronic games, and a small box of kiddy toys and books. Each kid, except the youngest, is responsible for his/her own gear. Family rule #1: You forget it, you do without.

"Family rule #2: Raid the pantry and fridge for basics; then head for the grocery store for provisions and ice (keeping list handy, budget $100 for groceries). Rule #3: gas up the van, check oil and tires the night before hitting the road.

"Friday. Gather up griping teens after school and head north on I-45. Depending on construction, accidents (in the van or on the freeway), and weather, we arrive at Huntsville State Park in a couple of hours, approximately 100 miles from home.

"From megatropolis to East Texas jungle, from auditory assault to deafening silence and noisy birds, from visual and olfactory pollution to the pungent smell of pine pitch and the lulling wavelets lapping on the lake shore glimpsed through dense tangles of greens. Houston, jobs, girlfriends, telephones, and weekend chores are light years away. Tents are up in minutes; kids scatter to check out the swimming, paddle boats, playground and hiking trails. I bask in aloneness. Fees for paradise: $15 plus boats.

"Burgers on the grill are followed by S'Mores. Foil-wrapped potatoes salvage the last heat from dying charcoal. Stargazing, night hiking, ghost stories, and giggles replace the radios and electronic toys that I have well hidden.

"Saturday morning we make Farmer's Breakfast: bulk sausage scrambled with a couple of the baked potatoes (cubed) and a dozen eggs. Served with salsa and wrapped in tortillas. Breaking camp, we continue on Interstate 45 to Buffalo, turn west on State 164 to Groesbeck, then north on State 14 to Ft. Parker State Park. The $2 entrance fee guarantees restrooms and a playground break. TrailMix, fruit, and thawing lemonade fortify us.

"From Groesbeck, we travel through Waco to Glen Rose (State 6 to State 144). We reach Dinosaur Valley State Park, pay a camping fee of $15, and enter rolling hills, covered with scrub, locust, and cedar. Setting up camp in record time, we pack sandwiches, change to swimsuits, grab towels, and set out for an afternoon of discovery. Beneath limestone cliffs, the Paluxy River has etched at layers of strata revealing dinosaur footprints waiting to be explored. Splashing in the shallows, swimming in the pools, hiking the nature trails, a little fishing, and the astonishment of sighting the head of a dinosaur above the distant trees. We forge toward the monster and discover not one but two, full-scale dinosaurs behind a chain-link fence. A short drive or a long hike takes us to Creation Evidences museum, also on the Paluxy, and provides another view of dinos in Texas.

"After an exciting and exhausting afternoon hunting dinosaurs, pre-cooked link sausage on the grill with Ranch-style beans heated in the can and reheated baked potatoes make a quick, no-fuss, filling dinner.

"Tired explorers sleep late Sunday, then breakfast of grilled cheese toast, reconstituted frozen orange juice, and fruit. After breaking camp, we stop in Glen Rose for gas. My deprived pioneers beg for soft drinks and their first junk food in ages. They sleep or read through Waco and stir for a picnic 100 miles south on Highway 190.

"Lake Summerville provides a perfect picnic spot for the starved, a chance for a jog, a swim, or a nap for only $3 before the final 75 miles home. Even teens will regret having to return, if only because of Rule #4: clean up before dark.

"Costs for the trip:

three tanks of gas	$ 90
groceries	100
entrance and camping fees	40
boating	20
Extras: charcoal, ice, milk, bread	25
Drinks, junk food	20

Total $295

"Balance: Bribe for pizza after van is cleaned and everything is put away."

My "penny-pinching" approach for a family outing won the $350 prize and a TV guest spot on local talk show featuring inexpensive things to do with your family.

Years later Chris and I returned to Creation Evidences Museum. Changes had occurred. The museum had been enlarged and the exhibits strengthened. We learned that human footprints discovered on the state-park property had been destroyed because the state could not justify or explain their being there and still cling to the "old-earth" theory.

Chris and I participated in clearing limestone slabs off of a trail of dino prints. We helped suction water off of the ledges and assisted men prying slabs loose. We then used small picks and brushes to clean the tracks found beneath the slabs. Unfortunately, on this dig, we found no human prints.

I began to study books on Creation and Noah's Flood that I bought from museum stores and checked out from the public library. My interest in dinosaurs and the Bible developed into a passion for the truth. An explanation was presented over and over that dinosaurs were created on Day Six along with other animals. Dinosaur babies, not adults, were included on Noah's ark. After the worldwide flood, these young dinosaurs and many other creatures could not adjust to the weather, temperature changes, and changes in vegetation, so they died out. Most of the dinosaurs were drowned, along with other creatures and humans. Dinosaurs, being heavy, would quickly sink and be rapidly covered with silt, thus fossilizing, while smaller creatures and humans would tend to float and rot, not leaving behind fossils.

Huge mammals—the leviathan and the behemoth—were cited in the Bible in the book of Job as evidence that humans and dinosaurs coexisted. The descriptions of these beasts correlate with dinosaurs, not with any other animals.

The movie *Jurassic Park*, and the children's movie series, *Land Before Time*, portrayed the parasorolophos dinosaur making trumpeting sounds through its horn. Dave's theory had become popular fact. I wondered how many other theories (educated guesses) were now being presented to the unsuspecting public as facts.

Part Three

A Jamboree

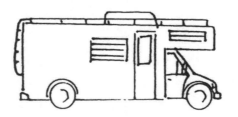

EIGHT

A Jamboree

My family wore out the pop-up camper, so we gave the remains away. My older kids grew up and moved on, so with fewer kids at home, we tried van camping with tents. But the van was cramped. My older boys no longer liked the challenge of tent camping. To them the novelty went out with Cub Scout uniforms. Cora still liked the tent, but I no longer liked the hard ground and claimed the van's bench-couch. My kids wanted to stay home with comfort, convenience, and TV, but travel and camping were still in our plans.

"I'm not getting older, just wiser," I told myself. Pop-up camping had been fun, but I didn't want another one, even with hydraulics, air conditioning, and a port-a-potty. I still wanted to travel, especially since I now had two grandchildren in Orlando, Florida. Somewhere there had to be a coexistence between roughing it and civilization.

I began to notice motor homes, camping trailers, and fifth-wheels on the highway. Maybe I'd get a camping trailer, I thought. It'd be cheaper than a motor home—comfortable, and self-contained. I scrutinized every make and model approaching on the Interstate. With a trailer or fifth wheel, I'd have to have a tow vehicle. Most of them were pulled with a pickup truck, but a truck wouldn't be big enough for my family. I dreamed of retirement, all kids grown and flown.

I picked up some RV magazines and searched the library. I eliminated trailers from my dreams because I figured that buying a motor home would cost no more than buying a trailer and a truck. And being a single, not-so-young female, I liked the security of being able to go from my driver's seat to my home without having to go outside and re-enter, especially in the rain or if I'm not sure of the security of the area. I could have the kitchen and bath facilities within a few steps of the driver's seat.

I discovered that motor homes were made in different classes. The Class A—a huge, rock-band, tour-bus-sized apartment on wheels with a diesel engine—was out. Some Class A's were complete with washer and dryer, closed-circuit TV for backing up, a satellite dish, and a Jacuzzi. Some were equipped with everything but driver and 75 gallons of diesel. A Class B was more like a van conversion. Self-contained, but much smaller than Class A's. The Class C was distinguished by a "cab-over", a peculiar overhang above the driver and front passenger seats. This design provided for a low-ceiling bed arrangement that gave extra sleeping space without adding to the overall length.

I scrutinized our neighbors in campgrounds. A huge Class A drove past. Glancing into the cab, I chuckled at the sight of a little gray-haired driver peering over the steering wheel. His co-pilot, a little gray-haired lady, held a gray mini poodle on her lap. He opted for a pull-through space; they gracefully disembarked through the living-room door. The couple wore matching, knee-length white shorts, pale blue, Ivy-League shirts, white tennis shoes with white socks and straw hats, hers with a blue ribbon. The poodle sported blue toe nails and a matching blue bow.

I guessed that her idea of roughing it would be a situation in which the linens didn't match. His would be a situation in which he couldn't tune in the satellite dish. I peeked over the top of my book as they set up.

After the basics of water and electricity were hooked up, out came the electric canopy. Slide-outs were deployed. He placed a large, indoor-outdoor carpet on the grass under the canopy and slid the latest design in lawn furniture out of the basement. She handed him a coffee maker, which he placed on a folding table and plugged into an outside outlet. They set up a little wooden corral for the dog, then stretched out on lawn chairs to enjoy TV while waiting for their dinner to microwave. Not my idea of camping.

We visited some RV sales lots. Before directing us to the back, pre-owned lots, we always had to pass the miniature mansions on wheels, with a price tag to match. My kids couldn't resist taking a peek. The salesman unlocked the passenger door and stepped back. Coming down to meet us were electronic steps. Watch your shins. Step up to opulence. To the right was a large, flat, leather dashboard, edged to keep goodies from falling off. This was the location for the navigator's lap top computer, the GPS (global positioning system), decorative souvenirs, and/or a vase of flowers.

The driver's and co-pilot's seats reclined. Their arm rests had recessed, insulated drink holders with a heating element. No cold coffee! The driver's cockpit was complete with a control panel fit for a small airplane. It had TV monitors for the remote, rear TV cameras to make backing this monster easier. We turned left through the living area. It featured a white leather sleeper sofa for guests, light beige carpet, and a pair of over-stuffed recliners that flanked a lamp table.

The dining area, with table and chairs, and TV, VCR, and CD players in an entertainment center, led to a kitchen with white terrazzo flooring, stainless steel sinks, microwave, stove and oven, large refrigerator with freezer and icemaker, coffee maker, dishwasher, and pantry.

The large, rear bedroom featured a king-sized bed, centered in the back with plenty of walk-around space, closets and dressers, TV, VCR, etc. And this model didn't even have slide outs—room stretchers that slide out through the exterior wall to make the interior wider.

A large bath had a skylight over a full-sized tub and shower. The toilet was, of course, of the marine variety but didn't look it. The rig even had a washer and dryer.

We picked up our chins and ask to be escorted to the used rig lot to look at Class-C rigs.

Late that summer, on my way to work, I noticed a dull green, ugly, Class C with a "For Sale" sign on it. I passed it twice a day for several days. It looked well broken-in. But I'm broke too, I thought.

"Just for the learning experience", I justified, as I turned into the driveway to check it out. It was a 1976 Jamboree, 21-feet long, and slept four very friendly people—two in the cab-over bunk and two on the convertible couch. The owner happily pumped up the propane, lit the stove-top burners, and turned on the generator and the air conditioning. He introduced me to the marine toilet, gray- and black-water holding tanks, and a tiny shower that leaked. He apologized that the refrigerator didn't work, "but it keeps food cold with ice", he reported.

I took the kids and went back for a second look. The rig had '70s orange carpet and a green and brown interior. Maybe it was nostalgia that motivated me, but we went for a noisy test drive. The owner's asking price was low compared to the new and slightly-used models on the lots. I began to daydream of financing possibilities.

A fact-finding visit to the loan officer at my bank should have discouraged RV fever. It didn't. I could finance the Jamboree without starving and could become an RVer now, not wait years until retirement. What temptation!

"Lord", I prayed, "Is this a good investment? Do you want me to have this one now?" I continued to pray and justified the purchase. I was excited, had apprehensions, and was challenged by my second home.

What a learning experience! Fresh water went into the tanks here, but don't drink it unless the tanks have been sanitized. We carried drinking water in jugs. The water hose hookup to by-pass the tanks went there, but I needed a regulator to keep from blowing up the pipes. The electric hookup, called shore line even though there wasn't a shore and it wasn't a line, got plugged in this little cabinet and then to the power box. Some outlets don't work.

The sewer drain hose goes where? Way under there where you have to get on your hands and knees and pull two little handles and hope nothing leaks. I made a rule. Whoever used the toilet had to empty the tank. No one ventured to use it. Campground restrooms were more than adequate. We never used the shower, either, except for storage.

The refrigerator worked fine like an icebox, holding a bag of ice and perishables. Except for sudden stops when the door fell off.

The lock on the side-entrance door repeatedly worked loose; the door came open at the most unexpected times. I added a chain and clip around the handle to hold it shut. The outside step often vibrated loose and popped out.

An egg-crate mattress was added to the convert-a-couch, but I still felt like the princess with several peas under me. The cab leaked just a little. I was scared of the propane stove and brought along my microwave and an extension cord. We preferred cooking outside on the grill, but those inevitable rainy days do happen.

On one of our first trips I ran under the guardrail at the entrance to a shopping center and cracked the roof air-conditioner cover.

My kids, like all kids, love fast food. While on the road we decided to use the drive-thru and followed signs around the back of a restaurant to discover a low roof over the carryout window. Thoughtful drivers behind me graciously backed up so this "crazy lady" could back up and avoid getting stuck under the roof.

My new experiences continued to pit hope and courage against ignorance. The Jamboree made a trip to Orlando with no excitement except that the speedometer went out, but that was OK since I preferred to drive slow, just in case. We took two Shelties and their puppy, Wilma—a gift to the grandkids. A rigged baby gate across the kitchen kept them from under my feet.

On the way back the alternator began to discharge. The headlights dimmed. By the time we reached Louisiana and found an exit from Interstate 10, I was worried. The rig stalled at a stoplight in a small, off-the-highway town. I nursed the RV into a service station, where the attendant gave me a jump and directions to a repair shop. Chugging down the road, the tough old thing let out a tremendous backfire and died. We jumped. The kids yelled, thinking we were goners, too. I coasted into a grocery-store parking lot. For the first time I used my road-hazard towing insurance.

The kids sang, "A tow, a tow, it's off to the repair shop we go!"

The wait was reasonable, with snacks from the grocery to ward off impatience. We were towed to a repair shop, where the mechanics willingly worked after hours to install a new alternator.

Our next few trips were uneventful, but then on a quiet highway in Missouri, on our way to Indiana, I heard a thud and a scraping sound. I quickly pulled onto the shoulder. The rear bumper had hit the pavement. What a racket with your bottom draggin'! We piled out. My kids began to speculate on what Mom was going to do this time. I sent Nick to get the rope with which we tied the dogs out. (My crew now included the two Shetland Sheepdogs.) We pushed and pulled the bumper off the ground and by looping the rope around the roof top railing, we were able to pulley it high enough to keep it from dragging. Cora announced that she could see daylight between the back door and the floor, so everybody rode near the front to keep the weight off our rear end.

I slowly inched down the shoulder and into the next town. Servicepeople at Wal-Mart gave me funny looks when I explained our problem but provided excellent directions to a truck stop with mechanics. Here a welder took pity on us and was willing to attempt a repair. He stayed after hours to weld the chaise where it had broken. His torch was too close to the gas tank for me, so I took the kids and dogs for a long walk. Long after dark he directed us to a campground.

We had discovered that many campgrounds did not have grills or fire rings for outdoor cooking, so on this trip I had carried our microwave oven. Our stopover at Mammoth Cave in Kentucky coincided with a rainstorm; hence we relied on the microwave. I had reluctantly given in to civilization. As we continued our travels, I experimented with cooking in the microwave most anything that could be cooked on the stove at home—not just baked potatoes and hot water for instant foods.

Our adventures with Jamboree taught me several very important rules for traveling with dogs. Never feed them in the morning before hitting the road or give them treats during the day. Only feed them when stopped for the night. Always carry plenty of plastic shopping bags to use to pick up after them and for cleaning up dog barf. A spray can of carpet cleaner and a whisk broom are a must, as are rolls of paper towels, a box of baking soda, and lemons.

After witnessing a wreck involving a travel trailer, I was glad my choice had been a motor home. The wind was strong as I began pulling out from a roadside rest area. I heard the squealing of brakes and the loud, grating scrape of metal. I watched as the wind caught a large, new camping trailer, causing it to fishtail. It flipped on its side, breaking the trailer hitch from the car. The car spun in a circle on the highway and ended upright on the shoulder, while the trailer continued spinning on its side down the highway.

Fortunately, it did not enter the line of opposing traffic. The trailer split open, spewing insulation and personal belongings onto the highway.

Neither the driver nor his wife was hurt, only panic-stricken. This was their first trip in their new rig. Thank God the propane tank did not leak and cause a fire.

1976 may have been a great year for the Bicentennial and for Jamboree, but. . . ..

The well-used, broken in, 20-year-old Jamboree had been a good beginner's rig for me. I had learning experiences that I could never forget. I had not gotten discouraged by the mechanical problems. After all, I could relate. I was not so youthful myself.

In 1998, retirement from teaching in public school became a reality. However, I took over a small, Christian school with which I had been associated for several years. Soon I became administrator, teacher, custodian, and bus driver of students in all grades from kindergarten through high school. With a self-paced, individualized curriculum, teaching was a joy. But I still dreamed of traveling.

Part Four

Traveling with Tioga

NINE

Tioga

The Jamboree had its finale. It was time to say, "It's been fun", and to look for a replacement. In the two years we'd "Jamboreed", we'd been to Florida, Indiana, Georgia, and many places in Texas. Jamboree taught me a lot about RVing and the difference between a lot-linked home and a house on wheels that could be a home. I now knew the difference between gray water and black water, what a shore line was, and other RV terminology. I had learned how to cook almost anything in a microwave and to use the refrigerator as an icebox. Traveling in Jamboree had increased my desire to roam, especially as my family at home decreased. All my kids except Christ were soon grown and on their own.

An RV dealer opened a new lot on the Interstate access road near my home. I passed it frequently, eyeing the shiny, new cottages on wheels. I saw it on the back of the lot. A Class C— newer, but not too new (i.e., expensive.)

The salesman explained that it was called Tioga. I liked the name. It was a recent trade-in—a 1988, 24-footer. This motor home had a double bed built into the back corner of the rig. The corner of the bed frame and mattress were cut off to allow passage along one side of the bed, where a bedside bath was situated. This meant the toilet and sink were about a foot from the side of the bed.

A folding door closed off the bath and bedroom. A shower was at the rear. It was too small for anything but storage. The couch made a bed, too. And so did the cab-over. The tiny compact kitchen housed a stove, sink, and a built-in microwave oven.

"On the road again, can't wait to get on the road again. . .." A trip to the bank, a trade-in deal, and we were ready to roll.

In January 1997 Chris and I acquired Texas Discovery Passports. These little books listed, by region, all the state parks in Texas. Each time we visited a park, officials stamped our passports. When someone visited all the parks in a region, the Parks Department sent a certificate and a colorful, souvenir patch. Chris and I decided to try to visit all 202 state parks in Texas. We also bought a Conservation Pass allowing us free entry into all state parks for a year.

Texas has it all. White sandy beaches, 'gator-filled swamps, jungle thickets, swelling hills, pine and hardwood forests that roll west across cedar and scrub, to cactus and sagebrush. Coastal plains, verdant hills, miles of prairie radiating to the compass points are rimmed on the west with hazy mountain peaks. Rugged, shear-cliffed and canyoned, the mountains appear as a moonscape. All of this is in Texas. If you don't like the scenery or the weather, drive in any direction—things will change drastically.

Driving from the city of Orange in East Texas to El Paso on the west, you are halfway to Los Angeles. El Paso to Orange is halfway to Jacksonville, Florida. The center of the southern United States is the Texas capital—Austin. Where else but in Texas can the adventurous RVer find this diversity?

By December 1998 we'd explored all the state parks "in the neighborhood", within several hundred miles, and made plans to explore the West. Chris and I agreed to exchange Christmas gifts with the family on Christmas Eve and to head West early Christmas morning. We watched the sun rise in the rear-view mirror as we passed through an unusually deserted downtown Houston on Interstate 10.

We stopped to have our Texas passports stamped in Kerrville State Park and then continued South on Highway 6.

"S" curves proceeded at 10 mile an hour with curves. Chris sat on his new skateboard and scooted from the front to back on the floor as we climbed and descended the hills. Seatbelts for a skateboard? I couldn't do anything but yell at him. I certainly couldn't pull over. A dropoff was on the right and straight-up cliffs were on the left. The climb continued up steep hills toward Lost Maples State Park.

A few years earlier we had spent a spring night here at Los Maples, tucked into a hidden valley of saw-toothed maples— the only trees of this kind in the state. On that visit we had hiked up the canyon to a small lake through a forest of trees putting on new, green growth. On this evening, in mid-winter, the trees were nearly colorless. Most of the golds, reds, and oranges of autumn had faded and fallen. The temperature was dropping too quickly for us to attempt anything more than a short hike to walk the dogs.

A supper cooked over an outdoor fire warmed us. We then were ready to add blankets on top of our sleeping bags. What an enjoyable change from Houston's muggy weather!

I forgot to turn on the heater, so at daylight, when the dogs, Sam and Lady, began their wake-up yips, I pulled on an extra pair of sweatpants and a heavy jacket before I took them out.

Frost coated the ground and crunched underfoot. The air was crystal-clear. Although we were in the shadows of the surrounding mountains, the inevitable sunrise illuminated a cloudless, turquoise sky high overhead.

I teased Chris out of his cocoon and into heavier clothes. Hot cocoa sounded good, but no water emerged from the faucet. Chris and I bundled up to check it out. The water hose had frozen solid. I feared that the connection was frozen, too. Using water from the refrigerator, I heated a cup full in the microwave and poured it over the outside faucet. Making sure that it could be turned off, Chris unscrewed the hose. Another cup of water heated in the microwave was poured over the RV connection. It thawed enough to disconnect. We left the hose in the weak, morning sun.

We warmed up with hot cocoa and instant oatmeal made with bottled water "nuked" in the microwave. Bundled up again, we walked the dogs and explored a beautifully frosted, clear morning. Pebbly frost covered the ground; a thick sheet of grainy ice crusted on the trash cans.

Walking along the edge of the woods, we noticed strange plants that appeared to have frosty, white ballet skirts at their base. I allowed Chris to pull up one of the thick, dry stalks so he could examine it further. We were astonished to discover that thin sheets of ice crystals had oozed from splits in the stalk to create a many-pleated ice skirt.

Yipping in pleasure, our dogs frisked in the frost. We kept well away from sleeping campers and tried to hush the dogs' interruption of the crisp stillness. The sun brightened the cloudless sky long before it appeared over the Eastern hills. Birds awoke and sang. Campers stirred up their campfires and made coffee. Oh, the fragrance of coffee on a crisp morning! And I don't even drink it!

We disconnected the electricity and prepared to continue our trip. The water hose was still frozen, so I screwed the two ends together and laid it out, stiff and crackling, on Tioga's floor.

We stopped at the ranger station and learned that the temperature was 23 degrees. This was the first freeze of winter. We asked about the strange plant we had seen; we learned it was called "freeze weed." During the first freeze the plant splits at the ribs of the stalk. Frothy sap is forced out to form the thin sheets of ice crystals that looked so much like a skirt. We were fortunate to see it, as the crystals melt quickly as the temperature rises.

Slippery roads slowed to 10 miles per hour during our trip through the steep hills. Deer along the roadway watched us warily with huge, dark eyes. Then they bounded across the roadway and into the underbrush and low, pin oaks. Chris discovered huge icicles clinging to the sides of shady cliffs. The rising sun's rays were blinding in the clear sky and caused the winter colors to glow.

Our next stop was Garner State Park. This old Corps of Engineers Park was one that my family and I had first visited when was a child. To tunes from a jukebox I had learned to ballroom-dance—with my feet on top of my dad's—on the old pavilion floor.

A new ranger station in a different location greeted us. I recalled our last visit here 10 years previously and discussed with the ranger the changes. At that time we had stayed overnight on a Saturday in May. Day visitors had left a mess of trash. Trash cans were overflowing; restrooms were dirty and trailed wet paper. Buzzards busily attacked the abandoned tables, cleaning up leftovers. Then I had talked with the ranger about the misuse of this once-beautiful park. That ranger told me of plans to raise fees to discourage masses of day users and to pay for better maintenance. We had agreed that overnight campers, as a whole, were conservationists and tried to take care of their sites and the parks.

The ranger verified that the raised fees had helped preserve the park in several ways. The flow of day users had been curtailed and the problems with trash improved, too. The new fees had helped provide for new camping areas and preservation of the original, old CCC buildings.

We drove around the park, investigating the clear, cold river. Dammed for summer swimming, canoeing, and paddle boats, it was much too cold now for wading. I showed Chris shallow, limestone pools used as small tubs and rapids that would knock you off your feet. We found the trails that I had climbed as a child and slid on my bottom to the bottom. On this day, the park was occupied only by quiet campers enjoying the beautiful valley, its clear, rushing river of white foam, and its green-walled cliffs.

In a small but busy town, I stopped in the left lane at a traffic light. A not-so-handsome stranger on my right waved at me, opening the door of his pickup. Visions of an RV-jacking flashed through my head. He pointed at my right, rear tire and yelled, "Flat!" I yelled back, "Thank you!'

The light changed; I eased over to the right. A mechanic at Wal-Mart just shook his head and pointed to a tire shop down the block.

Fortunately the tire was only low, or so I thought. The real problem was the inner tire of the duals. It had almost no air. A faulty valve core was replaced reasonably quickly at a reasonable price. The lecture was free: "You got thump 'um tires."

"I have no idea what you mean," I admitted.

"Drivin' that rig makes ya a trucker, and ya gotta do what the truckers do. Thump' em every mornin'." He demonstrated by pounding on each tire with a stick. Shaking his hand I thanked him for his advice and have "thumped" tires periodically every since.

Without contact lenses I'm nearly blind. I use bifocals for reading. I have even slept with them on occasionally when I felt insecure. When I got serious about traveling, I purchased a pair of trifocal glasses for emergencies, but I rely on the contacts and bifocal glasses and am super cautious when time arrives to remove the contacts.

The Tioga's bath sink didn't have a stopper, so I was in the habit of putting a towel in the sink, or I'd sit on the bed to take out my lenses. But one night when I got careless, my right lens popped out, rolled into the sink, and disappeared down the drain. I stared at the hole, one eye foggy. Gone.

I sat on the edge of the bed, knees touching the sink, and prayed. Where does one find a plumber at 9 p.m. in a state park, 100 miles from civilization? I would have to make a long, cold walk in the rain to find the park host's site and an even longer walk in the dark to the ranger station. It would be closed anyway.

To get intimate with the sink, I took off the remaining contact lens and put on my emergency glasses. I got a flashlight and peered down the offending orifice. I knew that I could drive with the trifocals, but that would mean admitting defeat.

Out from under the sink emerged the first-aid kit, toilet paper, and stuff. The flashlight revealed a white, plastic drain pipe leading down into a "P" trap. Hey, I'm good! More enthusiastic now that I remembered about "P" traps, I tried to find a way to remove it. Sitting on the bed, my chin in the sink, elbows jammed inside the cabinet, I tried loosening pipes. I tried kneeling, backside against the bed. I got so hot, my glasses slid down my nose. One ring thing unscrewed on the drain. The trap went away from me and through the back wall, but it was looser.

At last the trap was free. Now what? If the lens was in that nasty water, how would I get it out? I took the trap to the kitchen sink and very slowly poured the gray, yucky water into a plastic bowl. It was there! My beautiful contact, glittering in the waste! I fished it out, washed it in clean water, and soaked it in cleaning solution. Who said women are helpless?

On this trip the gas gauge didn't register. I estimated that I could drive at least 200 miles or 4 hours before I needed gas, but I didn't take chances and filed up every 150 miles or so through West Texas, where the gas stations were far apart. Gassing up near Amstid Lake, we headed north, northwest toward Seminole Canyon State Park on the Pecos River.

The possibilities of seeing Indian pictographs intrigued me. At a dry, dusty gas station, I got out my state-parks guide and was disappointed to read that the last canyon tour for the day started at 3 p.m. Without stopping again for much-needed gas, we arrived at the ranger station at 2:30, just in time to register for the last tour.

Our guide was a volunteer—a retired professor whose hobby was studying the pictographs for the Fate Bell Shelter. As he led us to the edge of the canyon, he described these pictographs as next best to the famous ones in Southern France. Past a sculpture of a Shaman, we went down natural ledge steps. I admired his hiking stick made from a polished sotol stalk. I envied him for having its support as the trail's descent became steeper.

A hike down steep flights of carved rock steps, most with hand rails, took us one and one-half miles into the canyon. Reaching the canyon floor, we walked out onto a broad, limestone terrace bordered on the right by a shear, cliff wall and on the left by the remains of a summer-dried stream and by the opposite wall. The guide pointed out a wind-carved cave in the distance, about halfway up the right-hand wall. Following a trail that crossed lines of brush, we climbed more rock steps up into the overhanging cliffs.

Then we climbed from the canyon floor to the floor of the overhung cave. The wind and flooding had hollowed out a long, open cave that Native Americans had claimed as a religious shelter and living quarters. Here we followed on a rubber mat-covered trail. The mats were to protect layers of rock rubble from erosion caused by visitors.

The guide pointed out various spirit paintings. We saw a mural of Shamans, recognizable deer, panthers, and arrows. Several areas depicted less-recognizable animals and humans. We also saw the spray-painted outline of a human hand. Was the artist merely playing when making this design, or did it have spiritual significance? Many paintings were so high under the cave roof that the artists must have used some sort of scaffolding or piles of rubble to reach these areas.

Another area of the cave yielded evidence of cooking fires and living quarters. A large stone near the drop-off edge of the cave floor was drilled with shallow depressions and had been used as a butcher block and as a place to grind grain.

As the sun began to descend beyond the rim of the cliff overhang, we backtracked toward the stairway. The return climb from the canyon floor to the rim was breathtaking in its beauty and difficulty. I had to stop often to "admire the scenery" and to catch my breath.

That night our campground was a high mesa that provided a stunningly clear view of millions of stars.

The following morning I stopped at the first gas station I saw—a tiny isolated building by the side of the dusty road, with one pump, two ranchers playing checkers, and a third acting as attendant. The gas prices were the highest on the trip. The clerk drawled that the distributor didn't like hauling gas to deliver so far from "nowhere" and wanted to close the station. I gladly paid, grateful for any gas, as we were many miles from Langtry.

We stopped in Langtry to visit Judge Roy Bean's Law West of the Pecos Museum and the Jersey Lilly saloon. I especially enjoyed wandering through the cactus gardens and being reminded of the names of those strange desert plants that I rarely see.

In the visitors center, a dried mesquite tree was adorned with desert seed pods, old bird's nests, and other strange natural objects proudly displayed as a "West Texas Christmas tree."

We crossed southwest Texas through Dryden (a most appropriate name) and Sanderson (another appropriately named town), due West into the blinding afternoon sun to Marathon. Sixty miles due South: Big Bend! What a name! The wilds of West Texas had been calling to me. And now, here we were, an over-55 senior dreamer, an 8-year-old boy, and two Shetland Sheep dogs in a 10-year-old motor home.

In Marathon, I topped off the gas tank and headed south. The seemingly deserted, two-lane highway had not changed. I looked forward to 60 miles of arroyos, cactus, sagebrush, and dry gullies with six- to eight-foot flood gages. The Chihuahuan desert. My third visit—and the magic was still there. This trip I tried using a tape recorder to tape my impressions.

Chris, tired of the desert, slept. Lady, the boss dog, snapped and growled at Sam from her hiding place under the small table. Sam, who acts macho but defers to the older woman, ignored her and jumped on the passenger seat to see out. I laughed.

I'm like Lady, hiding in the safety of a motor home rather than braving it in a tent. I thump tires, check the oil, and often pay for hookups so I have electricity. I admit it; I don't want to rough it. Yet like Sam, I want to see. I want to experience.

Maybe playing Paul Revere at camp Newana when I was a youth had left an impression. Travel gave me an exhilarating sense of emancipation, a sense of relief in the change from home responsibilities and cares. I liked the challenge of facing the new and of solving different problems. Not on my own but by relying on God.

Panther Junction appeared in sight. The parking lot and ranger station were extremely crowded. Most popular were the restrooms, the first in 60 miles. The main building had a topographical diorama of the park and a place to stamp National Parks Passports. Several seasoned hikers in high boots, shorts, dusty backpacks, and carrying aluminum hiking poles filled water bottles and registered for backcountry permits. Newcomers with unscuffed boots, stylish clothes from L.L. Bean or Lands'End, and high hopes of becoming experienced naturalists questioned the rangers. Others, like us, just wanted to experience from the security of campers the vastness and uniqueness of this wonderful place.

Checking in at Rio Grande Village, we set out to explore the sand slide. Lady had squished between the captain's chairs and struggled to get her fat self out. I made a mental note to exercise both of us. The trail over the mountainside and through the cane was much like I remembered. No snakes, this time. Chris squealed at the sight of the rushing river and had a great time skipping rocks into the rushing water. Impatient, I encouraged him along to see a surprise. The cave was so high on the mountainside that when I first pointed it out, his response was, "So what?"

We rounded boulders and approached the base of the slide. Chris yelled in surprise and began to climb. I planned to sit at the bottom in the shade and rest my senior self. Chris reached the top and yelled for me to join him. I probably wouldn't have attempted it, except that he kept disappearing from sight. I started to climb. On hands and knees. Two steps upward, one slide back.

This was getting me nowhere. I moved to the side of the sand where gravel was on the rocks and made better progress. Several kids passed me going up. I huffed and puffed. Chris joined them sliding down and climbing back up. I paused to watch (and to catch my breath). Up and down they went. Up I went, slowly. Was I out of shape! The climb was worth it though. I could brag that I made it and that the view was terrific.

We returned to camp and headed for the public showers, which were coin-operated. Even after inserting the necessary quarters, both men's and women's showers provided only icy-cold water.

Chris rode his skateboard while I did laundry. He met two boys and their father, whom we would meet again on our trip, and a girl whose family lived in a converted school bus for six months every winter. She was Homeschooled. Now there was an idea!

Chris showed off on his skateboard for a young lady who was riding a bicycle across the United States. She shared with us the location of a hike along the river on a boardwalk that led to the top of a bluff. From there in the late afternoon, we searched to see the tiny village of Boquillos, Mexico, south of the Rio Grande.

Leaving the Big Bend of Texas behind, we returned north to Fort Stockton to visit the old military fort. We wandered through reconstructed buildings to the recorded playing of taps. While here we learned that a star party was scheduled for that evening at the McDonald Observatory.

At dusk we made a long, slow climb up a narrow road to the McDonald visitors center. The parking lot and tiny building were crowded with families waiting in line for tickets to view outer space through the telescopes. Many of the families had young children along.

A beautiful, clear, cold dusk slid into twilight and inky blackness. The crystal-clear, moonless night was a perfect backdrop for untold millions of stars. Bundled in coats, caps, and gloves against the icy wind, people overflowed into the parking lot and grounds. An astronomer, using a powerful flashlight as a pointer, identified the constellations and a Russian space station in orbit, twinkling above the horizon. He explained that this observatory was the location of many astronomy studies because of the unusually clear atmosphere and the lack of interfering artificial lights.

By the time a full moon had risen, four telescopes had been set up. Long lines of cold visitors waited to rotate at each telescope. Our wait in line after line as we took turns viewing was worth suffering from finger-numbing cold. The largest, a 36-inch telescope, was focused on one edge of the moon. The sight was awesome. I could see a very bright, pitted, cratered surface of the moon, with a clean-cut, curved edge backed by the black sky. The moon appeared so bright that its reflected light hurt my eyes. Another telescope permitted a clear view of the rings of Saturn. The third was focused on Venus; a fourth gave us a view of the Milky Way.

Awed by our glimpse of heaven but getting colder as the night grew later, we reluctantly returned to the campground. Hot cocoa and popcorn from the microwave hit the spot.

Returning east early the next morning, it was time to fill the gas tank and check the oil at a small truck stop. I popped the hood release, got out, and couldn't get the hood to open even a crack.

I pulled the hood release again and inspected the hood again. Tight as a clam. From the garage a short, elderly Mexican mechanic watched with a grin. He walked over and slammed his fist into the center of the hood; it snapped open. I laughed and thanked him. He smiled, pulled the dipstick, and announced with a strong Spanish accent, "A quart low, ma'am."

"Thanks, I'll take a quart."

"Wait," he said, turning toward the garage. He returned with a quart of oil and asked if I had a funnel. I didn't but should have. Off he went again. He scurried, zigzagging from place to place—this time returning with a plastic soda bottle. A quick flick of his pocket knife took off the bottom of the bottle. The neck went into the oil filling place. A perfect funnel. Finished, he stuffed a paper towel into the bottle, wrapped another towel around it, and gave it to me. "You might need this."

Chris and I decided to try out the truck stop's cafe for breakfast. At the counter spanning the rear wall sat our mechanic. Chris jumped onto a counter stool next to him, spinning his long legs into the serviceman and me. We adults exchanged understanding nods over the boy's head. Chris insisted on a real trucker's breakfast: pancakes, eggs, sausage, and juice.

Chris asked me about telephones at each of the booths and then asked the mechanic. He learned that the truckers had to keep in contact with their offices, so the phones were provided and were also used as computer terminals.

Many truckers were using cell phones. I noticed that women were truckers, too. The mechanic asked if my husband was traveling, too. I answered "yes", even though "he" obviously was not with us. The gentleman then gave me a note with his name and phone number in case we had any mechanical trouble down the road.

Our return took us through Kerrville, a hilly area with many small antique shops. The Admiral Nimitz Museum in Fredericksburg was on our passport, so we planned a stop. Not being a buff for history—my worst subject in school—I guessed it was just another old fort. Why would a state park in Fredericksburg have that name? I couldn't recall the name in Texas history.

I was surprised to find a real, Old-West, frontier town with clapboard and stone-fronted shops that lined a wide, main street. Signs tempted me to explore several other historical museums. On a corner was the Admiral Nimitz Museum. looking like a three-storied, boardwalk-fronted hotel.

Ghosts of World War II greeted us in the foyer. Chris whooped, "War stuff!"

I was less impressed. Korea, Vietnam, Cuba, Kuwait, and Iraq had made me an ostrich. I nervously read the newspapers, watched the TV news updates, and prayed that war would never involve the U. S. again.

Chris was enthralled. We learned that the museum was a memorial to the survivors and dead heroes of World War II. Admiral Nimitz, one of the signers of the declaration of peace that ended the war, was a native of Fredericksburg.

Born only weeks after the bombing of Pearl Harbor, I was a war baby, but I knew very little about the war. Because my father's job made him exempt from serving, our immediate family was not dramatically involved. By the time I was old enough to hear war stories, time had passed; the stories were old history.

Chris, in awe, wandered from one display to another, mesmerized by displays of old photos of action and army equipment. I was stopped by photos of "Rosy the Riveter", children collecting scrap metal, war bonds, and grocery shelves with limited-rationed canned goods.

Infant memories struggled to the surface: Mother stirring orange stuff into white oleo to make "butter", gas rationing for our black club-coupe sedan. My brother and I had stood behind the only seat. I recalled my uncle in his uniform.

The weapons displays and model battleships called to Chris. Photos, newspaper clippings, and videos of actual newsreel footage reached my emotions that had never been stirred by history books. Choking up, I fought undetermined tears for war victims, soldiers, hatred, the loss of peace and security, and the destruction of lives, families, and property. I shuddered at Chris' innocence and his fascination with weapons.

Deeply breathing a sigh, I turned to follow Chris. Guns, photos of the atomic bomb blasts, model aircraft, uniforms, and medals fascinated him.

In front of a long, wall-display case we encountered a past-middle-aged gentleman standing at parade rest, staring, in deep thought.

Chris sighed and "ohh"ed and "ahh"ed over "neat, cool" weapons.

"That's the M-16 rifle I had," the gentleman mumbled to himself, pointing to one of the smaller rifles behind the glass.

"You were in the war?" Chris asked in awe.

He turned to us, misty-eyed, "Yes, at Guadalcanal."

Feeling his pain, I only answered, "Oh."

He breathed deeply and sighed to regain his composure. In a trembling, hesitant voice he replied, "I was in the Navy and on that island when they dropped the bomb on Hiroshima."

The man's emotions stopped Chris's chatter. He turned from the display and said to Chris, "I was just 16."

I stated, "I didn't think you could enlist that young."

"Couldn't. But there were ways." He paused. "My brother was in the Marines, sister in the Waves—a nurse, and Dad was in the Army. Well, I got in. Had to do my part." He told us that the previous summer he had taken his son and two grandsons to visit Pearl Harbor.

I wanted to question him, to hear more, but he returned to his private thoughts and shuffled into the next exhibit.

"Wow, he was really in a war. I want a gun and be in a war." demanded Chris excitedly.

I pulled him aside and tried to explain that real army and war are not like inter-galactic battles on TV. This was real and personal.

"Chris, you saw the movie back there of the bombing, right?" He nodded.

"It was horrible. An unbelievable explosion and atomic cloud. Millions of people were killed or burned horribly. War is not a game." I don't think he understood.

Outside the building we followed a path and a memorial wall that led to the entrance of a Japanese peace garden. How ironic it was to find a gift from the Japanese people in Texas. The Japanese government had sent ambassadors to construct a small Japanese House, gardens, and a Koi-filled stream as a memorial to the peace treaty signed by Admiral Nimitz.

I sat by the stream contemplating my worst school subject, history. "Rosy the Riveter," women on assembly lines wearing aprons over coveralls, hairnets, grease. No hosiery, nail polish, or makeup. Mothers trying to "make do". What was important? Family, yes. The "I-can-do" spirit. Independence. Women became head of the family. The men returned but women didn't want to give up a sense of worth, their newfound strength. Most wives voluntarily gave up leadership of their families but did not become subservient. They were the little women and the power behind their men.

My mom was always a homemaker. I was reared to marry and be a homemaker. I wanted college and my parents agreed because I could marry well. I was considered intelligent and a reasonably good student. I wanted an education because I enjoyed learning and wanted a career as a teacher. Marriage and children were in my plans, eventually. I was a Romantic; I was also hard-headed and independent.

I pondered how women's lives had changed after the war. Here I was, a single mother with 12 children, self-supporting and independent and loving it. My struggle for an education did not pay off with a high-salaried job but in self-satisfaction.

Perdenales Falls State Park. What an enticing name. I thought I had calculated just enough time to find it before dark. The long twilight of late December was misleading. We drove to Johnson City as the sun was setting behind scrub cedars and low hills.

The park turnoff from the state highway was well-marked, but now the sun was a memory. The road, a narrow two-lane farm road, rose over hills and fell into fog. How much further? I dared not try to read the map while driving in the dark; no place to pull over existed.

Finally. The headlights picked out a sign for the park road. I saw the entrance gate. Chained shut with a padlock! I eased the motor home to the far right and read a small sign by flashlight. "Closed for deer hunting."

What? My stomach growled. Chris grumbled. I griped. Deer hunting! Leave those "Bambi"s alone! Outdoors was so dark and desolate that backing down the narrow road to turn around was a stretch of nerves. Our only other option was to camp here on the road until daylight, but with deer hunters in the area, I wanted as far away as possible.

"I'm hungry, Mom!"

"Not now, Chris. Don't bug me." I tried to explain why the park was closed. I don't like hunting, hunters or hunting seasons, or guns of any kind. Chris, with that boy's fascination with weapons of all kinds, toy soldiers, and war movies, didn't agree. We finally did agree that the deer population must be kept in check.

The dark, lonely farm-to-market road crested a hill. We spotted a few distant specks of light. Civilization! Too hungry to cook, I splurged on burgers. Then I splurged for an RV park.

TEN

Caving

We had traveled from East Texas's Big Thicket to Big Bend, from the Rio Grande Valley to the Panhandle, and crossed the Hill Country many times. Now we made our first trip beneath Texas to see the wonders of Texas caves.

Longhorn Caverns was developed in the early 1930's and is one of the state's most popular show caves, because it is well-developed with elaborate lighting and is easily negotiated. Our guide was a native of the area, a marine-biology student, who had often visited the cave as a youngster. His mother was on the tour, so he gave us his best.

The cave originally had five natural entrances. All but one of these had been closed to prevent illegal entry and destruction of the cave. Although the cave did not have a great deal of formations, it has a long history. Archeologists had found the fossils of prehistoric camels, elephants, and bison and evidence of use by the Comanche Indians.

The remains of an Indian girl had been found. Bullet molds, guns, and evidence of gunpowder explosions from the Civil War era were traced to the manufacture of gunpowder by the Confederate Army. Legend holds that the outlaw, Sam Bass, used the cave as a hideout. Later, during Prohibition, the cave was used as a dance hall and "speakeasy."

We also heard a story of a kidnapped girl rescued by being hauled up a rope through one of the original entrances. Another story depicted the mystery of hidden treasure and lost maps that spelunkers today are still trying to find on special, treasure- hunting tours.

We learned not to throw coins into underwater wells, because the unnatural minerals caused contamination. Many caves today are "dead", formations no longer grow, because of contamination by explorers and the touch of human hands. I heard the guide speak of geological processes that formed the cave as taking thousands of years. Then he changed it to hundreds of thousands of years. If water seepage caused erosion of the original rock, what would a worldwide flood do? I wanted to learn more. I became hooked on caves.

Returning home, I shared photos of our trip with good friends Wanda and Brett. Here in Southeast Texas we have no caves. Because we are so close to the water table, a deep hole draws salt water. Wanda surprised me by her eager interest in visiting Texas caves. Her husband, Brett, teased that they had gone to Natural Bridge Caverns on their honeymoon and that she had a difficult time climbing all the stairs to return to the surface.

Despite Brett's threats to leave her in a cave, we began to plan a Texas caving trip. Caving must be contagious.

Traveling with Wanda, Brett, daughter Brandi, and their Sheltie, Missy, Chris and I and our dogs set out in search of caves. My friends were on a time schedule; it was August. A hundred miles west of Houston, thumping sounds alerted us. Was it the road? No, a blowout. A large church parking lot was available. We pulled over. The outside dual tire on the rear was very flat. Grateful for road service, we pulled out the awning, lawn chairs, and cold drinks and waited in the heat.

The blown tire had knocked off the sewer hose holder and a drain pipe. Brett picked up the pieces off of the road. Now we were hours behind schedule. Did we turn around? No way. Caving had become a calling.

Our destination was Natural Bridge Caverns near San Antonio. This cave was discovered in the 1960's. It was named for the 60-foot-long limestone bridge that spans the natural entrance. This cave was a show cave, meaning that it had been developed for visitors to enjoy and for the protection of the cave itself. Evidence of human habitation had been found here. The bones of a bear that became extinct 8,000 years ago had also been found.

The guide explained that the cave was a constant 70 degrees and that it was active, meaning that the formations were still growing. We were cautioned not to touch anything but the hand rails because the oils from our skin would damage the formations. This massive cavern is the largest commercial cave system in Texas and had some of the most spectacular formations. Some formations were 50-feet high. Stalactites hung clustered from the ceiling. Stalagmites grew upward from the floor. Where they met, columns formed. I was fascinated by the delicate, thin soda straws that hung like thin silver threads. Chris was amazed by the rare "fried eggs."

We discovered that caving was habit-forming and decided to follow a fellow caver's directions to the Cave Without a Name. We hastily checked maps and the time schedule and headed to Boerne.

From Interstate 10, homemade signs directed us through the tiny town of Boerne, then down country lanes, until we reached a pasture with a small stone building set off to one side. This cave was privately owned. It acquired its unusual name through a contest, when one entry stated that "the cave is too pretty to have a name."

Our small group was joined by two couples on a private tour. First we were shown the sink hole, full of Daddy long-legs, into which a rancher had lost a goat. He sent a hired hand into the hole on a rope to retrieve the goat; a small cave was discovered. In 1939, the owner blasted a new entrance down into the cave and added spiral metal stairs for access to the main level 90 feet below. Here moonshine was made during Prohibition. By accident some boys discovered a much larger room and a quarter-mile of fantastic formations. A rock wall with a door and a gate now protect the cave from intruders.

As we descended the old iron stairs, the guide pointed out cinderblock walls that had been used as reinforcement. He showed us flowstone that had been deposited on the wall. The thickness of the flowstone coating the wall was of a known date and did not correlate with the theory of ancient formations that take millions of years to form. This cave was still active; dripping water had continued the growth of formations.

Wanda asked the guide for an explanation of the quick-developing flowstone and the aging of caves. He replied that he had to go by a script from the owners, but that he, personally, leaned toward a young earth and that caves were formed rapidly through the erosion of flood waters. I wondered, "If dinosaurs could have lived before Noah's Flood, and millions of years weren't required for cave formations to develop, why are we taught that the earth is millions of years old when the Bible seems to indicate only thousands?"

At one time gravel had been spread on the floor to make walking easier, but now it was being removed so the cave would be in its natural state. A frozen waterfall of flowstone awed us. Cave bacon 22-feet long hung from the ceiling. Cave bacon is a formation like a type of thin, translucent drapery with alternating bands brown and white that did resemble thin-sliced bacon. One grouping of stalactites, called "Mary, Joseph, and Baby Jesus", attested to a Christian explorer. Thousands of soda straws and odd helictites, looking like strangely bent, angular and branching soda straws, led us to an underwater river. The guide and his friends had used scuba gear the night before to explore the frigid river. He explained how easy it was to lose all sense of direction in the blackness.

Here, we learned about another private cave, Sonora, recognized by experienced cavers as the most beautiful cave in Texas. We got out our maps again and headed farther West. Late that afternoon we turned south off of Interstate 10 following well-placed billboards advertising Sonora as the most beautiful cave in the United States.

Sonora had a small campground, visitor center, and gift shop. Early the following morning we entered the cave with a small tour. It exceeded our expectations for beauty. The formations were the most elaborate and fascinating I had seen. The beauty of this cave could not be exaggerated, even by a Texan. Almost every inch of the cave surface was covered with growing fragile formations: coral, crystals, stalagmites, and stalactites. We saw delicate and translucent dripping bacon and draperies. One of the most spectacular formations was the translucent Butterfly. Seven-and-a-half inches from wingtip to wingtip, the formation is still growing. Cave coral trees, as much as three-feet tall, and long, delicate helictites and six-foot-long soda straws covered walls, floor, and ceiling.

We all wanted to stay longer in this cave than the tour allowed, so we decided to take a second tour through a less-developed part of Sonora. We were not disappointed.

On our return to Houston, we detoured to visit Inner Space Caverns in Georgetown. This cave was accidentally discovered in 1963 when highway crews were drilling core samples for Interstate 35. Their drill bit dropped 26 feet into a void. The hole was enlarged; cavers rappelled in to explore a huge, unknown cave. Here they found the remains of mammoths, saber-tooth cats, and many other animals. Scientists dated the cave at 60,000 to 100,000 years old. How did they make that guess? Could the earth be that old?

ELEVEN

Carlsbad

Chris and I were now thoroughly hooked on caves. The following spring break we began a long drive through the Texas Plains due west past Fort Stockton then northwest into southern New Mexico to the famous Carlsbad Caverns. Oh, how I wished for Wanda's and Brett's company on this long trip through dry, desolate plains. But they had been unable to take the time off from work.

I chose a campground at White City near the entrance to the National Park because it was the closest; I wanted to tour the caves as soon as they were open in the morning. The rates were unusually expensive for water, electricity, and a covered table. The site had a small shower room with toilet but no other amenities. We paid for proximity to the caves. A large, expensive gift shop situated next to a hotel enticed Chris to spend his money.

We drove into the mountains to the cave entrance and gift shop to check out schedules and admission prices. We returned to the campground at dusk.

A brisk, cold morning beckoned us. At 8 a.m. we arrived at the Carlsbad information center just as it opened. Waiting to buy tickets we began a conversation with a man carrying a little girl in a backpack. His son, about four, and their grandpa talked to Chris. I commented that he would get tired of packing her. He shared that he had packed the boy since he was an infant and then began to pack his daughter. I was reminded of packing Chris many years ago. Now he was big enough to carry me!

Chris chose the natural entrance to the cave and three miles of hiking. The entrance had been modernized for safety so that it didn't look "natural", even though it was in the original location. Rock lined the walls and around the natural entrance, an arch 90-feet wide and 40-feet high. Flowering cactus flowed from crevasses in the rock walls. Swallows were beginning to return from winter migration and flashed from the dark recesses of the cave opening into the morning light, flitting to and from the walls to plants to the sky. Chris was disappointed that we saw only a few bats. They were still wintering in Mexico and wouldn't return until later in the spring.

We descended the steep, paved trail. We had no guides but saw many informational plaques. Hairpin turns wound the trail back upon itself. We encountered a long series of tight, steep, "S" curves. Metal pipe handrails and rock retaining walls helped us keep our balance. My legs began to tire. My calves ached.

The trail descended 829 feet in one-and-a-half miles of switchbacks. My knees felt the strain of braking against the decline. The air was damp, the trail slippery, the metal rails clammy. Near the bottom of the natural entrance the cave widened. We stopped, looked back, and saw sunlight filtering from the cave entrance high above. Mist rose toward the entrance, highlighted by streaming sunlight.

Now most of the trail was flat. Tremendous formations, huge, impressive and memorable, were at every turn. With names like Lion's Tail and Mirror Lake, Hall of Giants, King's Palace, and Queen's Chamber. The immensity of these underground, beautiful voids made me feel insignificant.

The trail led to the Big Room, a 1 1/4-mile loop of flat trails through formations so huge that they are seen from a distance, not up close. To me the formations were not as spectacular as those in Sonora except in their vast size and number.

Two hours in the cave, and Chris was getting tired and bored of formations. He wanted to buy souvenirs and to eat. We made a stop in the underground lunchroom and watched people pass who carried candle lanterns and lamp helmets for wild caving. I wished we had time for a wild-cave tour. Wild-caving involves crawling through small openings in the mud rather than walking on paved trails. The self-guided tour of the Big Room was fantastic and whetted my appetite for more caving.

Chris was reluctant to continue the tour. He was restless and tired. I could have stayed indefinitely. The formations were so awe-inspiring that I could gaze and videotape for hours more. But Chris would rush ahead, worrying me, then tire out and drag behind, frustrating me. We hiked for another hour but did not go on the King's Tour. I was disappointed, but this gave me an excuse to return.

We pulled out of White City and headed north to the town of Carlsbad. The narrow, two-lane road with limited shoulder on rolling hills was clearly marked "no passing." Rough pavement with tufts of prairie grass growing through Asphalt forced me to drive slowly. I heard honking behind and pulled on the narrow shoulder, expecting an over-anxious teen-ager in a pick-up truck or the driver of an 18-wheeler. Much to my surprise, I was passed by a bus-sized motor home. Most RVers are cautious and courteous. This one must have had an emergency.

North of Carlsbad, we found the Living Desert Museum. Here were trails planted with native vegetation and an arboretum. Rescued and rehabilitated desert animals were housed in adobe-style habitats. Vultures, eagles, and wild turkey were easy to see in covered shelters. Bears, wolves and deer roamed in large outdoor pens. Chris liked the snakes, spiders, and scorpions safely housed in glass-fronted cases. A large prairie-dog town permitted us a view of these funny, whistling creatures.

On our return from Carlsbad we made a stop at Monahans Sandhills State Park southwest of Odessa, a desert of 4,000 acres of sand.We rented a plastic, sled-like disc, climbed to the top of a ridge of sand, and Chris flopped on the sled to whiz to the bottom.

I watched with envy but didn't dare try risking injury so far from civilization. Chris delighted in an afternoon of sliding down huge sand dunes. Eventually one sand dune began to look exactly like the next sand hill, so we returned the sled and continued east on Interstate 20.

Fort Griffin State Historical Park appeared deserted. The visitors parking lot was empty. The day was warm, the air dry and dusty. Feet propped on his desk, the ranger appeared to be taking a nap. The park had no guided tours, but we were welcome to wander around the ruins of the old fort. He handed me a map.

An older gentleman in jeans, Western shirt, and Stetson appeared from a back room and introduced himself as a park host. He asked Chris if he would like to photograph longhorn cattle up close. "Go get your camera, and I'll take ya'll."

To our surprise, he retrieved an old, dented, Parks Department pickup and invited us to join him in the cab. He explained that he was a volunteer, a rancher from Fargo, North Dakota. He and his wife spent the winter months as volunteer hosts at campgrounds, glad to get away from Fargo. Fort Griffin was his favorite place.

He drove down a dusty park road to where a herd of longhorns were browsing or resting, scattered on both sides of the road. We appeared to be entering a vast prairie dotted with large mounds.

Our guide explained that the ancestors of this herd were originally rounded up by the late Frank Dobie in the 1920's. The rangy cattle with huge horns spreading to six and eight feet from tip to tip are living legends. Fort Griffin is their home range now, but often some of the cattle are sent to other state parks.

As we slowly approached, the huge beasts did not flee but seemed to recognize the truck. Some got to their feet, came near the truck, and followed as we crept through the herd. The rancher laughed at their docility and admitted that he fed them stale bread and Twinkies out of the truck window. I took videos as they stuck their damp noses into the camera lens.

Fort Griffin was established by the U. S. Army during the 1860's to help protect travelers in caravans of covered wagons heading to California. Troops stationed here campaigned against the Comanche Indians, who raided the wagon trains. A settlement called the Flat grew beside the fort and was temporary home to Bat Masterson, Wyatt Earp, and Doc Holliday.

Ruins of old Fort Griffin beckoned us across dry, dusty plains to peep through fallen, stone walls. One barracks had been restored and allowed us to experience the severity of frontier life. Several other buildings were in the process of being rebuilt. Tiring from the dry winds, we retreated to the motor home and continued east.

The day was beautiful and clear, with a cobalt sky. Temperatures in the 80's were cooled by a strong breeze. March wind gusts shook the motor home as we continued down Interstate 20. Ahead on the southern horizon Chris noted what appeared to be a dark red cloud. It grew larger and approached like a layer of red smoke. Soon we could make out red dust devils kicked up by the wind and passing over newly plowed fields. The dust was so thick I could hardly see ahead as the dust storm passed over the highway blown by a strong southerly wind.

I told Chris about the terrible dust storms of 70 years ago, when people tried to farm an existence in soil that blew away. My teeth felt gritty thinking about trying to keep house and cook with red dust sifting into everything. Gratefully, we left the dust devils behind.

The name, Possum Kingdom State Recreation Area, called to us as a great place to camp for the night. A lovely blonde young lady, with the figure and poise of a model, checked us in. We visited a small camp store to buy fishing gear for Chris. A senior citizen leaning his ladder-back chair against the wall told Chris how to find a good place to fish off of a rock cliff near our campsite. The lake waters were very low because of a drought, but fishing had been good. A heavyset man carrying a small radio emerged from a back room. He informed us that he had just heard a forecast for possible tornadoes from 6 to 9 p.m. The time at that point was 4 p.m. The sky was clear and blue, with a strong, welcome breeze. We bought some minnows so Chris could fish before the weather might change.

I mentioned that the ranger had said nothing about the weather when we registered and assured them that we'd watch the sky. The fisherman said he doubted the rangers would get advanced warnings in time to notify campers if the weather became severe.

Instead of selecting a site on the lake front, I convinced Chris that a site on an upper ledge would be safer. We backed in and hooked up, watching the clouds. Chris was unconcerned when I pointed out the cinder-block restrooms across from our site. I felt old, recalling that Chris wasn't born when we sat out a tornado in the KOA restroom.

Chris fished by throwing his line with a minnow into the lake and pulling it out immediately to see if the minnow was still there. Clouds, light and high, began to drift from the south. Surface winds from the east ruffled the still lake.

Chris impatiently moved up and down the lake shore, look-ing for a better place to fish. I sat with the dogs, on leashes, watching the sky. Fuller clouds began to form and move over-head. A cross current tugged on the dry grasses and stirred the lake. Now the clouds felt lower but were still white, not dark. Closer to sunset, as the sun glowed and reflected off the lake, cumulus clouds piled thicker and darker and began moving faster. Large patches of vibrant turquoise sky became blotted out.

I watched the clouds thicken and build toward the heavens. As the sun approached the hilly, western horizon across the lake, the air became heavy with impending rain. I called to Chris to gather up his fishing gear. Reluctantly he headed back to the motor home. I packed a flashlight, the cell phone, ponchos, and beach towels into a backpack, ready to evacuate to the restrooms if necessary.

Although the wind was now whipping the tops of the trees, it was not raining, so we ate a light supper outside at the picnic table, walked the dogs, and talked to a fellow camper about the approaching storm. As we spoke, the ground wind reversed directions. The temperature dropped at least 20 degrees. Our neighbor rushed off to her campsite.

Chris and I ran with the dogs to the motor home as large, hard drops of rain began to pelt us. The sky abruptly grew very dark, then green. I grabbed the backpack and ran with the dogs to the restrooms, through trees swaying in the high wind around us. The cinder-block building contained men's and women's restrooms separated by a covered passage. We ran to get under its roof. Chris, the dogs, and I entered the women's side. It was empty. Hail began to bounce off the metal roof. Sections of translucent, green roofing admitted a small amount of fading daylight. Rain pinged, drummed, then pounded on the roof. The lights flickered. Lightning flashed. Thunder rumbled and crashed.

During a lull, I stepped outside into the breezeway and watched the sky glow from green to yellow under a canopy of dark clouds. Trees whipped back and forth. The rains returned; the sky darkened again. We sat on the restroom floor with no company but the dogs, who whined and stuck to us like cockle-burs. In less than an hour, the storm had blown over. The winds became a breeze. We returned home in the twilight.

TWELVE

Key West

By November 1999, Chris (now nine), and I had visited 150 of the Texas state parks, from Port Sabine to Atlanta to Big Bend to the Valley. We were ready to return to Florida.

Feeling brave, I invited my mother, in her 80's, to join Chris, Nick, and me on our trip there. We spent a few days with my daughter, Colleen, and her family in Orlando. Colleen, her son, Devin (eight), and daughter Chelsea (five), all their gear, and two bikes joined us to travel to the tip of Florida. Would this multi-generational trip work?

Our first night out we pulled into a beautiful state park on the Gulf Coast south of Tampa. While registering, the ranger suggested that we check out the campground first because mosquitoes had invaded the area. We were tired and assured him that nothing could equal Texas Gulf Coast mosquitoes. We hooked up the Tioga and slathered in repellent. As predicted, the biters were BAD! We hurried to the showers, liberally reapplied repellent, and killed time in a screened recreation room. Supper was by microwave. I didn't dare tempt the tormentors by cooking or eating outdoors. We played board games and read until bedtime, disappointed that we could not explore the park. Those Florida mosquitoes must have migrated from Texas!

Our route crossed the northern Everglades on Highway 41. Interstate 75 had been shut down because of swamp and forest fires. Reaching Miami we headed south on Highway 1 to Key Largo, crossing over a very long causeway that originally had been a railroad bridge.

We pulled into a campsite at Long Key State Park. Our neighbors on the right were partying around a bonfire on the shore. On the left was a new, domed tent but no signs of occupants. Mosquitoes were hungry here, too, so we stayed indoors and went to bed early.

Colleen rose before dawn, doused herself with repellent, and walked down the beach to photograph the sun rising over the ocean. Grandma, grandkids, and the rest of us got up with the sun, doused ourselves with repellent and went out to explore. Passing the neighbor's campsite to the left of us, I noticed a thirtyish man standing stiffly, a coffee mug in his right hand, his left hand behind his back in a "parade rest." I had not heard him return during the night and was curious.

The kids happily rode bikes back and forth. I stole peeks at my neighbor while puttering around. He stared at the tent as if it were the enemy. He walked purposefully to the back of an SUV (it had not been there when we went to sleep), unlocked it, and lowered the tailgate. Carefully placing his coffee mug on the tailgate, he stood gazing at the interior as if he had never seen it. Methodically he arranged a few things, walked to the tent, and stood looking at it.

Our neighbor was dressed in a pressed, bushman-style khaki shirt, tucked into clean, pressed khaki shorts, hunter green knee socks and clean white athletic shoes. He looked like a model from L.L. Bean. He contemplated the tent. Again. Walked back to the rear of the car, again, careful not to kick up the sand. He picked up his coffee mug and returned to stare at the tent.

I was fascinated. Was he a novice camper? Was he here on a dare? He had no fishing equipment, no lawn chair, and no barbecue grill. Where was he during the night? Surely he hadn't slept in those clothes, so he either got up before dawn, or else he had not been in the tent at all.

I was so interested in watching him do nothing, not even sit on the picnic table to drink his coffee and look at the sea, that I decided to spy. I adjusted the blinds in the motor home so that I could watch unobtrusively from inside.

Mr. Fastidious squatted in front of the tent. Very slowly he pulled out a sleeping bag, stood, and shook it several times. He folded it crosswise and placed it on the picnic table. Realizing the table was sandy, he brushed it off with his hand, washed his hands, dried them on paper towels that he fetched from the rear of the car, and shook out the sleeping bag again. Then he refolded it and placed it on the table.

Seeming to be waiting for inspiration, he refilled his coffee mug from a Thermos and stood at parade rest, looking at the tent. Finally he set the mug down and very deliberately pulled the rods out of the domed tent. It fluttered to the ground. Laying the rods on the table, he made sure they were lined up evenly. Next he picked up the limp tent, shook it gently, and shook it again and again. The tent was folded several times like a sheet and placed next to the sleeping bag.

Now he faced the ground cloth. He walked around it.

Again. Retrieving a wisk broom from the back of the car, he squatted to sweep off the cloth. Then he carefully knelt on it and picked off specks. Again he swept it off. Mother and Colleen had joined me spying. We giggled as he folded the ground cloth once the long way, side to side, and walked around it to make sure the corners were perfectly matched. Now the exposed top was swept clean and the cloth smoothed flat. Around he walked, making sure nothing was out of line. He picked off a few specks. Creasing the center, and with much care, he folded the cloth in half, aligned the corners, swept it again, and walked around a few more times.

By this time we had all eaten a hearty, cooked breakfast and cleaned up. His cloth was folded up small enough to be picked up, but first he checked to see if each edge of each layer was even and that the corners matched perfectly. He stood back, scrutinized it, looked over at the table, walked over, and patted his tent to flatten it. He inspected the tent bag. And shook it.

Our neighbor did not seem amenable to receiving help, so I kept watch. He poured more coffee and sipped it, reflecting from tent to folded ground cloth. Obviously he wasn't sure what to do next. Then, decision made, he carefully unfolded the ground cloth, making sure it was flat and smoothed out after each unfolding. Next he took the tent, shook it out, and laid it on the ground cloth, meticulously lining up the sides and corners. Now he folded the tent lengthwise, swept it off, and repeated the same careful alignment he had preformed with the ground cloth. Finally he rolled the tent up tight enough to fit into the bag.

Placing the tent bag on the table, he noticed the poles. Out came the tent from the bag. Back on the ground cloth it went, in reverse, just as carefully as it had been rolled up. I wondered if the tent was borrowed or rented or had sentimental value. Now he dampened a sponge at the water faucet, careful not to wet his shoes, and wiped each tent pole, rinsing and squeezing the sponge before handling the next pole. When he was satisfied that the poles were spotless, he lined the poles up with their ends perfectly even on the end of the folded tent. He carefully rolled the tent back up with the poles inside and placed it back in the bag.

Since Neighbor had already made executive decisions and gone through the routine of folding up the ground cloth, you'd think he would be more confident. But, no, he repeated the walk-around, sweep, fold, match corners, crease, etc., etc. With a final brushoff he picked up the folded cloth, shook it, and laid it on the table, turning it over so he could brush off the other side.

Camping chores done, Neighbor carried the cloth to his car and returned to pick up the tent and take it to the car. He poured more coffee, looked at the folded, but not rolled, sleeping bag. Instead of rolling the bag on the table, he carried it to the tailgate of the car, shook it several times, and finally began rolling it up on the tailgate.

108

During this procedure, all seven members of my multi-generational family had cleaned up, dressed, eaten, cleaned up breakfast, made beds, gone for a long walk, loaded the bikes, disconnected, and were ready to pull out. As we drove by, Neighbor was using a mini-vac on the floor of his car.

On the way back to Orlando, my family made a secret purchase. They surprised me with a small metal model-T with the convertible top down and filled with artificial daisies. The little crank in front of the car wound up a music box that played "King of the Road." They sang "Queen of the Road" as they presented it to me and thanked me for the trip. I cherish it and the memories it brings.

THIRTEEN

The East Coast

Family legends spoke of a remote town of Weishample in Pennsylvania. Here was located a tiny church reportedly established by our great, many-times-great, grandfather, a circuit-rider preacher. Not being a historian, I had not tried very diligently to research the story, so my little brother, Alan, must be given credit for reconnecting us with our family history.

Several years ago Alan, a Baptist pastor in Louisiana, made computer contact with the pastor of the small Weishample Church of God. We learned that the church, established in 1853 by our great-great-grandfather, precluded the town. Alan; his wife, Pat; their son, John, and our mother were invited to visit with the Yankee pastor and his wife. They were treated royally and enjoyed their visit.

Alan preached in the 100-year-old church building. The following year, the Pennsylvanian pastor and his wife visited with us in Louisiana and preached in the Southern Baptist church. We became fast friends.

I now had an excuse to visit the East Coast and Pennsylvania, with a detour by way of Orlando to visit Colleen and her family for a week. Colleen and her children had a trip planned to Asheville, North Carolina, that coincided with our continuing on up the East Coast. So early Sunday morning she led the way as we caravanned north through Jacksonville and Savannah. All the kids rode with me.

Hot, muggy air was sucked into the open windows. The air conditioner would have felt terrific except with astronomic gas prices, I was conservative and left it off. Chris and the two grandkids were ganged up behind me in the breeze from the windows. A few drops of rain splattered on the windshield.

"What's that funny smell?" asked Devin, my co-pilot.

"It's probably the rain on the hot pavement."

"Oh, no!" I checked the gauges. "The temperature gauge just went to HOT!" I pulled on my headlights and flashed them on and off. Colleen pulled off onto the shoulder; I headed onto the grass behind her. Steam rose from the hood. The smell was stronger.

"Let's get out," I tried not to yell, herding the kids in front of me and out the side door. I grabbed the dogs' leashes and joined the kids with Colleen off the shoulder near the tree line.

"What's wrong?"

"I don't know. We smelled it and saw steam. You kids stay there." I got a pair of gardening gloves that I use for dumping the sewer and pulled the hood latch. Water dripped from the raised hood. It was actually hotter and damper than the climate. I couldn't see any busted hoses.

"Must be the radiator."

"I'll get the chairs," volunteered Chris, an old hand at road trouble.

"Good thinking. Get some water and stay in the shade of those trees." I got my cell phone, the road service's 800 number, and the map.

We guessed we were about 10 to 15 miles north of the South Carolina visitors center, but we could see no signs.

I called, but had a difficult time hearing because of the fast traffic rushing by. It was 1:15 p.m. The dispatcher wanted to know my cell number. I couldn't remember it. I never call it. Where were we? I wasn't sure. I asked Colleen to see if she could find a town on the map. Sweat stung my eyes.

I went outside, but the dispatcher couldn't hear me because of the traffic. The motor home was now a sauna. Sweat coated the phone. I was put on hold and panicked that the phone would die.

At last the dispatcher returned as my battery weakened. The weak battery caused the phone to crackle. The dispatcher promised to locate a wrecker. I couldn't charge the phone with the engine off. I didn't have a lighter adapter. The dispatcher told me to call back in a few minutes. We waited in the hot shade.

Frequently consulting my watch, I called back in 10 minutes and got a different dispatcher. While I was on the phone, a Police officer drove up. Colleen told him we were in contact with road service. He said he would be cruising all afternoon and would watch out for us. We enjoyed warm water while we waited in the limited shade.

I called road service again and got another, different dispatcher. She couldn't find the original call, so I gave her all the information again. The traffic got heavier. No one stopped to aid in our rescue. The police didn't return. The kids complained—hot, restless, and bored. We moved our chairs to stay in the shade as the sun moved to the west. A few clouds provided no relief.

Colleen and I agreed that she and her kids should continue on their trip. I promised to call her cell phone later. Chris and I moved the chairs again. We attached a sign, "please call police", to the rear of the motor home. Wind from the traffic pulled the tape off. It began to rain more than a few sprinkles. The highway steamed.

Whenever the sun broke through the clouds, we lost all shade from the trees and moved to the little shade beside the motor home. I didn't like being so near the freeway traffic.

Chris begged to go home. Okay, I sympathized. I just wanted to get off the freeway. The phone died as I tried once again to reach road service.

The engine cooled off, but the traffic was so heavy that I was afraid to go in front to check out my ignorance. We agreed that we couldn't stay here on the highway all night, so I pretended to know what I was doing and started poking things

under the hood. The hose from the overflow tank to the radiator had blown off. I pushed it back on and filled the tank with
water. Closing the hood we prayed that the engine would start
and not blow up.

The engine did start. We crept down the shoulder until I
could merge with traffic. We passed mile marker 15. Now I
knew were we were! The thermostat gage swung to HOT! I
pulled off onto the grass and shut down the engine.

"Chris, stop kicking the dashboard. I'm worried enough," I
said.

"I didn't," he denied.

"What then was that bumping? Did you hear it?" We scrambled out the side door, adrenaline racing. The thumping subsided. My racing heart calmed too.

Checking the state map again I figured out that I was about
three miles from a rest area. Chris and I agreed to try for it even
though it had begun to rain heavily. After the engine cooled, we
poked along for about two miles on the shoulder.

The gauge registered hot again. We stopped again. The
bumping, bubbling, boiling subsided. Waiting for the engine to
cool, we agreed that we would be safer to spend the night at the
rest area than on the highway, so we crept up the entrance ramp
to an almost-empty parking lot.

My sketchy plans were to see if I could locate a trucker
there who would let me use his cell phone. If not, we could
always sleep in the rest area and ride our bikes into a nearby
town in the morning.

A pickup towing a fifth-wheel camper was parked nearby. I
pulled alongside, prepared to beg for help.

"Look, Mom, there's a wrecker!" Chris practically shouted.

"Where? I said.

I got out and went toward the camper. As I rounded the truck's
cab, I heard the driver say, "No, I didn't call for a wrecker."

I called out, "Are you looking for someone to tow?" It was
now 4:30 p.m. and drizzling.

The driver looked over my rig and said, "I've been chasing you down. How did you get here?" I explained that after three calls, with the phone going dead, and the traffic noise, I was afraid that the dipatchers had never gotten enough information to send someone. I told him we decided to find a safer place to spent the night. He commended me for getting off the freeway, even though finding us had been more difficult. He spent about an hour adjusting the wrecker's towing bars, chains, and lights, and disconnecting Tioga's drive train. Chris and I climbed into his cab and we were off, retracing our route from Savannah.

The wrecker driver, James, said that he was taking us to Tim's Wrecker Service that had a mechanic on Sunday duty. Just as we turned into the truck yard, rain began falling again. It then started pouring. We ran for the garage. The rain fell in torrents. Thunder and lightning kept us under cover for more than an hour. We were made to feel welcome while we all waited it out. During a lull in the rain, around 7 p.m., James was able to back the wrecker with Tioga under a shed roof and replace the drive train.

The rain returned, slackened, and returned in a downpour. Water rushed over the parking lot, inches deep. At last a mechanic was able to turn Tioga around and get the front end under the roof. Chris and I went "home" in Tioga to make sandwiches for supper while the mechanic performed his diagnosis: a burned-out thermostat.

"We'll get one in the morning," he said.

The mechanic hooked us up to the business' electricity. We gratefully turned on the air conditioner. Finally the rain stopped. Chris, the dogs, and I camped where Tioga was sitting- —in a safe, fenced area with a night watchman.

Morning dawned with a clear sky. Chris and I walked the dogs around the neighborhood while the mechanic ordered parts and worked on Tioga. That afternoon, we drove past the place on the freeway where we had broken down 24 hours earlier.

Washington, D.C.

Our trip itinerary included a visit to fascinating Colonial Williamsburg, where Chris and I spent two days exploring the historic town. Then we were off to Washington, D.C.

I wanted Chris to experience our nation's capital, but I was not looking forward to attempting to drive in its traffic. Searching through a KOA directory, I discovered that the KOA at Front Royal, Virginia, offered a tour of D.C. with a shuttle from the campground. A phone call confirmed reservations for Tioga and for the tour.

At 6 a.m. on the morning of the tour, we were met by a small but elegant bus, its driver, the tour guide, and one other tourist. Leaving the driving to an expert in Washington, D.C., was a very wise decision.

I didn't know that Washington had two traffic loops, each going in opposite directions. Traffic there made Houston's traffic look like a drive in the park!

The guide took his three charges to all of the monuments, the Capitol, the White House, and to our choice of Smithsonian buildings. He was informative and personable. At the Iwo Jima Memorial a veteran gave Chris a photograph of the memorial. Chris' favorite stop was the Museum of Natural Science, because of its dinosaur fossils and of course its gift shop. We returned 12 hours later exhausted and well-educated.

Then we went on into Pennsylvania, through highway construction. I read this caution sign, "Slow Down. My Mommy Works Here!" That made an impression on me.

Weishample, Pennsylvania

Weishample, Pennsylvania, was marked with a village sign but was so small that it had only one crossroad, a tiny store, a cemetery, a few homes, and the Weishample Church of God. We turned around in a farmer's drive in order to photograph the sign to "our" village. I showed Chris the old spelling of our family name.

Our distant grandfather had been a circuit-rider preacher who had established the church as well as several others in the area in the mid-1800s. When the first stone church building was built, it was named after our ancestor, with our family name slightly misspelled. The village took on the name of the church. The original building was later torn down and replaced by a wooden structure. As the tiny village grew and the roadway built for horse and buggy was widened to accommodate automobiles, the road encroached on the church building. In the 1950's the church was moved to its present location on a hill a mile from the crossroads.

My first impression was that this beautiful, white clapboard chapel topped with a spire, on the crest of a hill covered with yellow flowers, belonged on a postcard.

We had met the pastor and his wife in Louisiana but had never visited them in Pennsylvania. They met us at the church and treated us as family. They gave us a tour of the church, of Amish Country, and of an anthracite coal mine. We were treated to a Yankee cookout in the tiny backyard of their quaint parsonage. The pastor invited me to park Tioga under the trees at the back of the church near the outdoor arbor.

On Sunday we attended services in the little church with about 20 elderly members. We spoke in amazement of how technology, particularly the Internet, had allowed my brother to first contact the pastor of this church we had only heard about in family legends. The congregation, some of the few citizens remaining in this shrinking village, were equally amazed to meet descendants of the person for whom their own church was named.

With regrets that we could not stay longer, Chris and I departed. It was time to return South.

Skyline Drive

The northernmost entrance to Skyline Drive along the crest of the Blue Ridge Mountains is just south of the Front Royal KOA. The narrow, winding Skyline Drive was everything I had read about, with dips and steep climbs. Overlook stops permitted us beautiful vistas stepping into the hazy distance. Lunch at a visitors center was followed by a hike with the dogs. By mid-afternoon we had entered the Blue Ridge Parkway, an extension of Skyline Drive.

Rhododendrons and mountain laurel were in late bloom. Traveling sightseers were slowed in the late afternoon as I negotiated tight curves and steep grades at less than 30 mph. I felt like a mama duck leading a passel of ducklings, so as soon as enough shoulder was available I pulled over to let cars pass. A pickup truck stopped ahead of me.

The driver, in his 50's with a gray beard, wearing shorts, T-shirt, ball cap, and sunglasses walked back to Tioga. He asked if I was looking for a campground and if I had reservations for one. Yes, I was wondering where to stop and no, I had no reservations. Didn't think I'd need reservations in the middle of the week.

He introduced himself and said he was owner and operator of a private campground. He went to get brochures from his truck and invited us to stay. He had a bumper sticker for the camp on his truck. The camp was not far, he said. He showed me the location on my map and suggested that I could follow him.

Since the campground seemed to be near my present location, and the closest national park was quite far, I agreed to use his camp and to follow him. He turned off onto a gravel road with a very steep decline into tall trees and brush. The road wound down with tight switchbacks. It became more narrow; the long, back end of Tioga appeared to brush the mountainside on turns. We dropped into shadows of the mountains. I became scared. Where was he leading me? How could I have been so naive and stupid! I couldn't turn around. We had passed no houses. Suddenly, the brakes got soft.

I flashed the headlights, pulled to the far left by a wall of rock, and stopped using the emergency brake. To the right was a dropoff into the forest to a dry creek bed. I was more afraid of Tioga's brakes slipping and of our plunging into the unknown than I was of the stranger. I passed the cell phone to Chris. I tried not to scare him and told him to lock the doors when I got out to ask the man for help. I popped the hood latch and took Lady with me. She barks at strangers and is very protective. Chris put Sam on the driver's seat.

What if we are stranded? Robbed? Or worse? The man walked back. I prayed, "Lord, how did I get myself into this mess? I was so stupid to follow him. Please, have pity on us and get us out of here."

A car emerged from the opposite way but didn't stop. I kept Lady on a tight leash while the man checked the brakes and used his cell phone to call the campground for someone to bring brake fluid. I listened carefully to his end of the conversation. Nothing seemed weird.

When the brakes cooled, he checked the brake fluid. It was fine. The brakes had just overheated from the descent. We waited about 30 minutes more for help that didn't arrive. I tried the brakes. They were still soft but held better since they had cooled off. I was afraid to wait out here in the wilderness any longer. The shadows deepend.

I decided to drive in first gear and descend very slowly until the road leveled off. If necessary I could use the emergency brake. I was much too scared to try to stay here isolated in the growing darkness. I followed the truck while I carefully applied the brakes. With my heart in my mouth we went down the twisting, turning, narrow, gravel road. At last, the road finally leveled off. We passed a gravel turnoff and appeared to be going west. Then we turned right onto another dirt road. No civilization. No road signs, but this road did seem to be a little more traveled. At last we passed a few small houses. Where was he leading me? I saw no campground signs. Abruptly the road emerged from the trees at the camp. I let out my held breath. I had been praying without ceasing.

The campground was small with a few, pull-through sites. It had only a few vacancies, as most sites seemed to be occupied by long-timers.

Nerves frazzled, hot, and tired, we hooked up and turned on the air conditioner. A short hike with the dogs lifted the gloom of the mountain shadows. Chris found a large, muddy pond full of tadpoles, which he had to catch and house in a small cooler to take home.

Showers, dinner, and early bedtime gave me ample time to contemplate our adventure. My trust in God deepened as I recognized that only He had delivered me from a potentially dangerous situation. I learned a lesson about needing to pray—not *after* I messed up but *before* making decisions that could get me into trouble.

Part Five

Going with Gus

FOURTEEN

Gulfstream

We returned home in mid-June from our East Coast adventures. Tioga was experiencing what appeared to be transmission problems from mountain climbing, failing brakes, and various other mechanical ailments. With TLC Tioga would serve us for short trips, but having worn out a second motor home, I determined to take at least a year to shop for a replacement. With a trip to Alaska in mind, I carefully prepared a "wants" list.

I preferred a Class C, so that Chris and I each could have our own space. It must be at least five years newer and about 24 feet long. Much longer, and I would have to pay a lot extra if we took the Marine ferry on the Inside Passage to Alaska. I would insist on a booth dinette, because the tiny table in Tioga was not large enough to serve two people; I wanted space to use as a desk.

A convertible sofa would be nice, but I'd prefer a real bed for myself. I did not want slide-outs—room extensions that slide out—or an entertainment center. An awning would be a plus.

I was on several dealers' sucker lists from previous "just-looking" visits. On July 1, I received an invitation to a Fourth of July Recreational Vehicle Sale-ebration and barbecue. The timing was off by at least a year, but my list was ready, so Chris and I went "looking."

Chris boarded a mega-bus, while I bypassed sales people and walked in the July heat to the pre-owned lot. There was only one Class C on the huge sales lot that was close to anything on my wish list. Most of the other pre-owned motor homes were buses or were almost new, with only slightly reduced prices.

An alert salesman walked over and offered to show me a 27-foot Gulfstream, Ultra 102, 1994 model.

"Too big", I told him.

"Nothing shorter on the lot in this price range," he replied, opening the Gulfstream's door.

Nice interior, except that I disliked mauve. A booth dinette! And a convertible couch. Great head room in the cab-over. The rear bedroom had a queen-sized bed. Bigger than what I needed, but with walk-around space and great under-bed storage. A definite plus. Then I saw it. The bathroom had a real door! Tioga had a accordion-type door that never stayed shut. Even though I knew we'd rarely use the tub-shower except for storage, I was impressed by a bathroom with a door.

Chris climbed in and spotted a TV-VCR mounted in a high cabinet. He was sold. My list said no entertainment center, but this was just a small set. Should I consider buying, without looking around? Chris didn't care that the generator worked and the roof air would run while we drove or that the cab-over bed was easier to climb into. He was sold on the TV. I convinced myself that the Gulfstream met most of my specs, except that it had no roof storage or ladder, but it had more than adequate basement storage. Gulfstream was longer, at 27 feet, than I had planned on, but that extra length allowed for the bigger bedroom. It had no ladder for a bike rack, but I could add a rack to the trailer hitch. And it did have a new awning.

Of course the salesman reduced the selling price just for me, just for today, and offered me a trade-in allowance I couldn't ignore—more that I'd paid for Tioga two years earlier. This was a great deal, except that I wasn't sure I was ready to buy, so I stalled and said that I had to talk to my bank.

A week later, I exchanged Tioga for the Gulfstream and loan payments. Two weeks later Chris; my daughter, Cheri; and her two impish sons, ages 3 and 4, took a shake-down trip to Kentucky to visit their other grandmother.

Grandkids. Love 'em or leave 'em—home that is. The two little monsters refused to stay under seatbelts. Their mom was just as stubborn and hard-headed as were the boys. She wouldn't reinforce my seatbelt rule—insisting that she was watching them.

I prayed a lot on that trip. First, that we wouldn't have an accident and they wouldn't get hurt, and second, that if I got stopped, she would be issued the ticket for not having them under seatbelts.

The boys discovered that by climbing up the back of the driver's seat, they could get into the cab-over. I doubted that it was legal for them to ride up there, but I sure wasn't having them climbing around my head. Grandma got mean! I pulled over, yelled, and laid down the law.

Late July temperatures were reaching into the 100's. We stopped early and pulled out the awning, but it did not shade the living area. I pulled down the roller shade behind the couch. It stuck half way down. The opposite shade came all the way down, but the top edge came partly disconnected from the roller. Good enough for one night.

In the morning we duct-taped the shade to the roller. Now it wouldn't re-roll at all. The other one hung-up halfway down. Everyone had an idea for fixing them. The tape came un-done. We re-taped. Leave them alone!

Frustrated, I'd rather drive with them at half mast and forget modesty at night. That night I took the rollers down and discovered that the heat had caused the original glue to melt. The previous owner had taped the shades. Now, although the roller was sticky, neither the shade nor duct tape would hold. The plastic rollers were too dense for staples or tacks. I could not get the little pins to go back into the gizmos on the wall to re-hang them, so the rollers and shades ended up on the floor beside the bed.

The solution seemed to be to replace the rollers with wooden dowels, nails in the ends to hang them, and cloth curtains that could be pulled shut or tied back.

At a lunch stop, I walked around and opened the side door, to be greeted by a naked three-year-old. His wet shorts were in one hand, his underwear in the other. Fortunately the carpet didn't need changing, too.

On the return trip from Kentucky, the boys' other grandmother was with us. I laid down the seatbelt law; she upheld it. We took the Natchez Trace, winding and scenic, and calmer than the Interstate. Cheri lay down with a headache. Lucky girl. I bribed the boys. Lie down and play the quiet game, but do not go to sleep! We Grandmas needed quiet time. I promised that I would get ice cream if they were quiet. Amazingly all my passengers went to sleep.

On this trip I practiced prayerdriving—especially for patience with the little ones and with their mother. I was grateful for the opportunity of owning a reliable motor home, years before I thought I could justify one. I was enjoying traveling and having new experiences, but I felt a calling to do something for God. What was it He wanted me to do? I could be a campground host in a state park. That would be fun, but I'm no preacher. How could I witness?

On Mission

My brother, Alan, has been a Southern Baptist pastor all of his adult life. I had difficulty accepting my pesky little brother as a preacher. Although we didn't live close enough to visit often, I learned that he not only preached a meaningful sermon but was a well-regarded pastor.

Fall of 2000 was life-changing for me. Mother mentioned that Alan was planning to take a group from his church in Louisiana on a mission trip to Mexico. At last I saw a way to serve the Lord with the motor home. I called Alan and asked to go. I think I heard hesitation as he explained the purpose of the trip: construction, cooking, witnessing, and children's programs. He politely tried to convince me to farm out Chris, because he didn't think Chris would be able to handle the poverty in Mexico. And I heard a little concern about his group of adults relating to Chris.

I assured Alan that I was serious about going, working, and witnessing, and that Chris and I were a package deal. He believed that the motor home would be an asset, since the mission station was under construction and facilities were primitive. Alan sent me an itinerary. I sent $100 ahead for the purchase of food and began to clean closets for clothing and linens to donate.

Chris and I had done some clowning and made balloon animals at our church. I restocked balloons and asked one of my students to help me with conversational Spanish. The youth at our church made Power Band bracelets to supplement the ones being made at Alan's church. Many individuals donated clothing, linens, and household items for us to take.

Mexico Mission

The Saturday before Thanksgiving I expected the group to arrive from Lake Charles around 8 a.m. and had donuts and coffee ready. Houston was unusually cold, with a near-freezing drizzle. 9 a.m. They were late. I fretted.

The cold, misty rain slackened around 10, just in time for the Louisiana caravan to arrive. Brother Alan and Russ led the parade in Russ's truck, pulling a U-haul trailer loaded with a washer, dryer, and two stoves. A refrigerator was standing upright in the truck bed. Joey and Phyllis pulled in next in their truck, pulling a flat-bed trailer packed with donated building materials and a large sink, many 50-pound bags of rice and beans, and clothing and other donated items under a flapping blue tarp. Six other volunteers left the warmth of a mini-van to greet me and store their gear in the motor home before heading inside to warm up. These six strangers and another volunteer that we picked up later joined Chris and me in the motor home. Chris positioned himself and his Gameboy in the overhead and was quiet around the strangers.

I was elected to lead the way and to get us around Houston. After negotiating the Ship Channel toll bridge, I accidentally led the others in running another toll booth in the fog and heavy rain.

By listening to the others' conversation, I learned that Alan had known the missionary couple, Bonnie (a man) and his wife, Carol, for many years, but he had never gone into Mexico before to help them. This trip's primary purpose was for the men to work on completing construction of a mission station, a cement-block building that would be a home base for others. We women would help cook and would witness to the women and children. In the evenings at different locations, the Mexican pastor, Rolando; Bonnie, and others would show Christian videos in Spanish.

Bonnie and Carol had a small home in Pharr, near McAllen. They led our caravan to the New Life League International Mission Station south of town for the night. Here we went over our papers with Ken, a retired missionary. I had a non-negotiable title for the motor home from my bank but was told that I might be asked for a letter from the bank giving me permission to take it to Mexico. I had gotten Chris and myself passports and brought a copy of guardianship papers, hoping to make things easier. I learned that the Mexican officials might question me about permission from his absent parents.

We were all shocked to learn that 17-year-old Ashley's papers had been left in the van parked in my driveway. We had no way we could get them. Ashley was particularly excited about this trip because she had been studying Spanish in high school. She was devastated that she could not cross the border. We joined hands and prayed together for an answer.

A Mexican pastor, a U.S. citizen, was visiting with us that night. He went home and returned with his 20-year-old daughter's birth certificate. He would take Ashley with him as his daughter when we crossed. What a dilemma. Should we lie about Ashley's identity or let the devil defeat her and keep her from witnessing? Our group had mixed feelings, but after prayer, we agreed that Ashley should be given a chance to go. If lying were against God's purpose for her, then she would be stopped at the border.

We made our last trip to Wal-Mart for bottled water, joking about leaving civilization for a week. My new friends bought new batteries for Chris' GameBoy and commended him for being so patient with the old folks.

Very early the next morning after a Sunday devotional, Bonnie gave us explicit instructions for crossing the border and added that each time he crossed, circumstances were different. We should be prepared for delays and frustration. We gassed up all the vehicles and exchanged dollars for pesos. The rate of exchange was 9.6 pesos to one dollar. I helped Chris to quickly figure out cost in our money by explaining that 10 pesos just about equaled one dollar; therefore he could look at a Mexican price and divide by 10 to see what it would cost him in American. He liked the idea of all those centavos and funny paper bills.

Crossing over the International Bridge, I parked. My group joined the others from their trucks inside the empty immigrations building. We felt some security in numbers with Ashley's "father", Ken, and Bonnie as translators. The one Mexican official, getting tired of our long line, handed us a stack of visa applications. We did not experience any problems with visas and re-boarded the motor home.

Someone in uniform looked in through the window. I was waved through the non-declare lane, probably because he didn't want to deal with so many people. We had been warned that they could ask us to empty everything out the motor home for a search.

We let out a collective sigh of relief, because the Mexican government did not like Americans bringing clothing to the Mexican people even though many were destitute nationals with little money for food or clothing.

I parked in a large, dusty lot with the others to get a vehicle permit. Ken led me to a small building to wait in line to get the forms and to have Texas insurance papers copied for a couple of pesos. Then he walked me to another small building, where I had to stand in line without him. I pushed the copied papers under a glass, where they were inspected and stamped. Because of the glass and my very limited Spanish, I couldn't understand what the clerk wanted. He made a side-to-side motion with his hand on the counter. Okay! He wanted my credit card. For a fee of $13 on the card, they had a record of my American address and a way to find me if I did not return the car permit or left the motor home in Mexico. This man was very serious.

Ken led me back to the first building to wait in another line to buy Mexican liability insurance. For six days of coverage my cost was $50 U.S. It was worth the money, since we were traveling 100 miles from the border into the interior. I had heard many horror stories about vehicle accidents and Mexican police.

After a quick, late, sandwich lunch, we loaded up. I followed Bonnie and the two pickup trucks away from the International Bridge and away from known civilization. The streets were narrow, the traffic fast, and the signs in Spanish. What would being a missionary on my own have been like? I had no map and no idea where we were going except that it was south.

Leaving the border towns, the two-lane road had enough shoulder to pull over to let others speed by. But most natives drove in the center, straddling both lanes. Signs read 80 KLM.

My limited math guessed the speed to be 55 MPH. Neither Bonnie nor the nationals paid much attention to the posted speed limits.

Thirteen miles from the border we were stopped at a checkpoint. A uniformed officer entered the side door. We all waved our visas and said, "*No habla espanol.*" He waved us past, but he too could have demanded that we remove everything from the storage areas.

One hundred miles past open range land, we saw tiny, tin or block farmhouses with small gardens. Here and there a cow or horse was tied near the road to eat grass. We passed many small herds of goats tended by boys on foot and a few large herds corralled by youths on horseback. The long drive gave me ample time to pray for our success in witnessing and in helping the Mexican people. I also prayed for our safety.

Passing small block buildings that made up a town, Bonnie turned off the narrow highway onto a dirt road. To the left was a deserted plaza with cement walkways, a statue of a man on horseback, and a few deserted venders' stands. Further on were small shacks in dirt yards, with a few chickens scratching here and there.

Bonnie pulled through an opening in a block wall and gave me directions to back into another opening. I did as instructed and then got out to survey the mission station.

We were engulfed by small children wearing sweaters or jackets against the cold, but few had on shoes. They wanted to help carry boxes and bags, for they knew that candy, or a few pesos, would be their reward.

Chris and I stood looking over the unfinished, block building that looked too new and large for its surrounding neighbors. The kids stopped and gawked at Chris, so large to be so young. We set to work, first chasing pigeons out of the building. The ceiling was only rafters; the eaves were open. Studs defined interior walls. The bathroom had two uninstalled toilets and space for showers. The main room had plumbing for a sink, several large tables and homemade benches, and boxes and bags of building materials.

This room was quickly emptied of everything and swept. A stove and the refrigerator were unloaded from the trucks and installed. We women were set to work preparing dinner.

The neighborhood kids attached themselves to Chris and followed him like baby ducks. A very personable little boy, Gordy, was constantly underfoot, wanting to be of help and to be rewarded. He invited Chris, through signs, the universal language of kids, to go to his house next door, where he lived with his grandmother and six sisters. Chris soon had the run of the neighborhood. Language was no barrier.

While the men continued to work in the building, Chris and I and two other volunteers dressed as clowns, paraded the dirt streets with balloons, and drew even more kids to the station. Nora, an English-speaking local, led in singing familiar Christian choruses in Spanish. Bro. Alan then led, as Nora translated, the plan of salvation, using the colors of the Power Band bracelets.

As dusk descended, Carol fed us a quick dinner while Bonnie tacked up a sheet on the outside wall for a movie screen. He began showing a children's Christian song video in Spanish. That settled down the mob of kids. As soon as we ate, we carried our benches outside for the many adults who had braved the cold and had walked up to watch another Christian video.

Pastor Roland led singing while playing his guitar. Alan spoke a short sermon that was translated. He then turned the service back to Rolando for more singing and an invitation. Several people came forward for prayer.

Monday was a work day for the men in the station. We women cut vegetables, packed rice and beans into small bags for distribution to the families, organized supplies, and helped in the kitchen. That afternoon, we clowns were driven to Pastor Rolando's tiny cinderblock church in another tiny dusty village. Here we were inundated with children of all ages who arrived for "globos", (balloons), bracelets, and to be told, "*Jesus te ama*." We teased them with small, happy-face finger puppets and quickly made friends. Most of the children were dressed in many layers of castoff clothing against the cold wind, but were without shoes.

As dark descended, a sheet was hung on the outside wall of the church; benches were drug outside. A video was started for the children; we guests were invited to sit around a table consisting of a couple of sheets of plywood on saw horses. We were served a meal of homemade tamales, beans with tripe and chilies, and cola in glass bottles. The tamales were excellent, but the beans were so spicy hot that most of us could not eat them in spite of the cold weather and warm cola.

Tuesday was a repeat workday at the station. Chris discovered a tiny mercado (grocery store) across the dirt road. Here he could buy gum and "penny" candy.

I agreed that he could shop if he shared with the children, who followed us everywhere. I snooped around the one-room shop, roughly half the size of my bedroom at home, and discovered a small, school Spanish dictionary. It cost me $2 U.S. and became a very useful souvenir.

More kids saw us return from the market and ran to us. Chris shared his gum and made new, instant friends. I asked one of the older girls, in my limited Spanish, "*Que es libro?*", showing her the book.

"*No es libro*", she corrected me. "*Es dictionario.*"

I chuckled to myself at my ignorance. Then I asked her if she had "*libro en casa.*" (at home).

"*No en casa*," she replied. "*Libro en escuela*" (school). How sad, I thought. These children have no concept of books being in their homes. They only associated books with the school that they don't bother to attend. School, I learned, was free for the first four grades. After that parents had to pay. Many children don't go at all. Those that did attend went in shifts. One group went for four hours in the morning. Another group attended in the afternoon, but most wandered the streets or stayed home.

Phyllis and I sat in the motor home and cut vegetables for dinner. She confessed that she and the others had been skeptical about having the preacher's sister along. How should they act?

I laughed. "You were worried about me?" I'm not stuffy, certainly not preachy. That's my brother's job. I do speak my mind at times, but I don't think I'm pushy, I don't care about making a good impression. She assured me that I had passed the test and that they all were glad to have Chris and me there.

On Wednesday I cooked hamburgers on an outside grill and Dutch-oven cobbler for our lunch. Then we returned to Rolando's church. More than 80 children came to see the clowns and to hear from Nora about God's love. Between 20 to 30 children responded to the invitation to pray the sinner's prayer. Rolando and Nora counseled with each of them, including Nora's 10-year-old, daughter Ana Karen. Our hearts were bursting.

Thursday was Thanksgiving. Work on the building stopped at noon for a traditional turkey dinner that Carol had prepared and brought frozen from Texas. Several nationals had been invited to eat with us. One young couple had a baby boy about four months old. I asked to hold him and then asked his name. Carol took me aside and explained that he had no name. Traditionally babies were not named until after six months of age, because the mortality rate was so high that many did not survive. I could not shake the sadness as I walked outside comparing my home to the stick and plywood shacks, dirt-track road, and ragged children waiting patiently for our leftovers.

Someone called our attention to two young boys sitting on the tailgate of one of the pickup trucks. One boy had on a Power-Band bracelet and was explaining to the other boy the colors of the beads. Those little seeds we had planted were sprouting.

Thursday night we had more to be thankful for. We traveled about 60 miles to a very poor village to show videos with the help of a generator. Whereas the mission station had electricity and a few hours of running water, this village had neither. The plywood shack that was used for a church consisted of two rooms with dirt floors and a tin roof. Our hostess fried fresh fish for us outside over a wood fire—her only kitchen. We were treated as family even though we couldn't speak each others' language. I was humbled to share their meal around a sheet of plywood with goats, chickens, dogs and puppies, cats, and a huge pig underfoot.

On Friday after closing up the station, we drove to a border town to shop and be reintroduced into civilization. Before we reached the Texas border, we discussed a return visit in the spring. Bonnie collected our visas because they were good for six months. We vowed to return before they expired.

Crossing back over the border, I hit the outside mirror on the passenger side. The force pushed the mirror support into the door, shattering the window glass. Fortunately the window was down, and the broken glass remained inside the door panel instead of cutting anyone. Unfortunately the weather was still cold; the plastic we tried to tape over the window blew off, so my passengers wrapped themselves in Mexican blankets. Strangers a week ago, sharing so much, we became close friends.

FIFTEEN

Missions Minded

Before the Mexico trip, I had been evaluating my life's goals. Here I was, over the hill, semi-retired, and single. My kids were reared, except for Chris, and I was free to do for me. But is that what I wanted? I was more determined than ever to travel to Alaska in 2002, because I'd be celebrating my 60th birthday. This was to be my gift to me.

I sat on the floor of the motor home with a vacuum hose, trying to get all the spilled rice and beans up out of the crevices and gum unstuck from the carpet. I'd changed on that trip to Mexico. I still wanted to travel, but now my focus was different. I saw what a difference I could make in other peoples' lives by volunteering to do what needed to be done.

I had never considered being a missionary. I certainly couldn't preach or sing, but I had learned that cooking, cleaning, and sacking beans was just as important.

I had been blessed in triplicate. Learning from Jamboree, Tioga, and the Gulfstream, called Gus, how to be independent and self-sufficient, not relying on anyone but God. I wanted to use Gus and whatever talents I had for God's glory.

Chris and I shared our experiences in Mexico and the video I had made with our church and our school. I had retired from teaching in public school in 1998 and had taken over a small Christian school that was situated literally in my backyard. For the past several years, I had been administrator, teacher, custodian, and bus driver for the school. The pay was poor, but the learning environment and student body were excellent.

When a date for our return was set for the first week in April, my students' parents agreed to let their kids have another spring break so I could close school and go to Mexico. Parents cleaned closets; soon my house looked like a resale shop with donations for our trip.

This second trip was blessed by several newcomers, including Karen, a young woman from my home church, and several different people from Alan's church. Jack had broken his back in a diving accident when he was 19 and was paralyzed from the waist down. He used a wheelchair and a specially equipped truck. Amy met and married Jack several years after his accident. She was shy and timid, a perfect compliment to his boldness.

Our caravan to the valley included Russ' truck, now with a camper cover over building materials; Jack's truck loaded with more materials; Joey's with a loaded trailer; a van; and my motor home, with Karen and Chris bringing up the rear.

We spent the night at the New Life Mission Station again and visited with Ken and his wife. Ken was now blind with diabetes and could not travel with us. We met the Martins, directors of Valley Baptist Academy in Harlingen. I had brought several boxes of discarded school materials for them to use in their ministry.

Early on Sunday morning after breakfast and devotional, we exchanged dollars for pesos, filled our gas tanks, and again crossed the International Bridge. Two of our returning missionaries' visas had been misplaced, so they had to reapply and pay for new ones.

Jack could not find his wallet with his driver's license and birth certificate. He searched his wheelchair and his truck. We prayed, determined not to leave him behind. At last Amy found his wallet, way under the driver's seat in his truck, under some clothing. Prayers were answered.

While waiting for instructions, several travelers sat with me in the motor home. Amy asked to use Gus' restroom facilities.

I didn't realize she was still there when I started up the motor and heard a scream. She thought an earthquake had occurred!

This trip I was prepared with a letter from the bank, permitting me to take the motor home into Mexico. No one asked me for it. I had proof of insurance and my driver's license ready for copying. Because I couldn't understand the charge, I just held out some pesos and hoped the man was honest in selecting the right coins.

In the second building I waited in line with my papers for an unusually long time for an early Sunday morning. My turn arrived to go to the glass-fronted window. I felt "experienced", until the uniformed national asked for something. I said *"no comprendo"* and asked for someone in line to help. A lady tried to explain: "a paper". What paper? I showed him the bank letter. The clerk shook his head, "no." He showed me a green paper. The lady told me he wanted mine like that. Digging in my baggie of papers, I did find a green one. He accepted it and proceeded. Then he did the side-to-side motion with his hand; I now knew that meant credit card. This time the charge was $17.

Karen joined me to walk back to the first building for Mexican insurance. No one was behind the window. The copy machine operator and his buddies indicated *"un momento* (one moment)." The time was 10 a.m. Some time after 11, a young man entered with a carry-out box that steamed and smelled delicious. An early lunch? Still we waited.

Bonnie and Russ arrived very frustrated. Russ had been asked for the green paper, too. He was turned away when he couldn't produce it. Bonnie explained that the paper was a receipt for turning in the vehicle permits on the last trip. He usually wasn't asked to produce it, because the information was supposed to be in the computers. He had not told us that this paper was important and to keep it. Bonnie tried to control his agitation as we pondered the situation. Neither Russ nor I remembered actually getting that green paper last time. Out of the habit of being a pack rat, I had stuck everything in a baggie.

Around noon the insurance official and his helper showed up. They asked in sign language the value of the motor home. He calculated that my cost for six days would be $90 American. I balked. Six months ago I had paid $50. He calculated on a notepad, mumbling in Spanish. I wrote a reduced value on the pad. He re-figured. Now it was $70 American, cash. I pulled out my policy from the last trip and showed him the $50 charge. He shrugged. I paid the $70 rather than risk an accident and going to jail.

Joey arrived for his insurance. The other official had not even asked him for that green paper! Bonnie and Russ drove about 30 miles to the city of Matamoros, where they woke an official, and then got his secretary to go with them to a closed office to get a copy of the green paper. It was a costly trip in time and money. While we waited, we ate lunch and prayed for this trip that was starting out so badly.

At last we all pulled out of the parking lot and into traffic. I relaxed with a little confidence from recognition of the area. I brought up the rear as the lead vehicle began to merge into the left lane and then into the left-turn lane. Suddenly a white compact sedan sped past me on the left dirt shoulder and cut in front of me. I slammed on the brakes. I had not experienced Mexican traffic problems on the first trip except for the disregard for speed limits and stop signs. Was this a preview of things to happen later?

The narrow, two-lane road had no shoulder, just a dropoff. An 18-wheeler, with another diesel tailgating him, was speeding toward me over the center line. I hung on to the wheel, held my breath, and moved as far right as I dared without going off the road. We came too close to being sideswiped. I prayed a sigh of relief. Later Jack, who had been following, congratulated my driving. My right rear dual was off the road.

Later, on the same road, with a steady stream of oncoming traffic, a truck towing a long trailer pulled alongside me to pass. I slowed as quickly as I dared. He cut in front of me. An oncoming car flashed his lights and honked furiously. Other drivers in the oncoming traffic also honked their frustration at the near accident. I was grateful that I hadn't needed that insurance.

Arriving at the mission station, we were met by old friends and the kids that followed Chris everywhere. I figured I could relax a little and began to hook up. On the first trip we had to rig a sewer connection with a piece of cut PVC pipe because the distance to the sewer drain was too far. This time I had brought a connector for the two hoses. As soon as the release valve was pulled, the connector burst, releasing stinky black water. What a mess! In went the valve and out came the duct tape and the bleach.

Our ministries on this trip were similar to the last, with many re-acquaintances with old friends. The nameless baby now had a name and was healthy. Nora's daughter, Ana Karen, had become a Christian and was now leading other youngsters in singing for the services. Gordy and the other kids attached themselves to Chris and took him around the neighborhood or climbed into the motor home if the door was not shut.

One afternoon seven kids tried to help me package beans and rice. They really wanted to help, but I had to do a lot of sweeping after their efforts. I got out Bible-story books in Spanish and had the kids help me read. With crayons and paper that I had brought, they drew pictures for me and helped me with my Spanish. I couldn't help noticing a new boy with bright red hair. He was about 12 years old and became attached to Chris, too.

On this trip the temperature reached the mid-90's. The heat was oppressive. The wind blew the sand constantly; we felt drained and gritty. The town's electricity suffered brownouts, so rather than risk burning up the motor home's air-conditioner, we suffered with a small fan. Water was scarce. On Thursday the town received no water at all.

After several days of grime, Chris, Karen, and I tried taking turns at military showers, using water from Gus' tanks. I got wet with cold water from the shower hose, turned off the water, soaped up sitting on the back of the tub, leaned way over and soaped up my hair. Then a quick all-over rinse. If I had been any fatter, I would not have fit in the tiny shower.

To keep pigeons out of the attic, the men planned to close off beneath the eaves of the building and to seal up the gables. However, pigeons were already roosting in there. Gordy volunteered to climb into the low, sweltering attic and get them out. He wiggled in like a lizard and was soon hanging out the open gable, dangling a pigeon by its legs.

Chris rescued the pigeon; the kids helped gather the other young birds as Gordy chased them out. We made a gift of the birds to Gordy's grandmother. She proudly put them into an old wire cage to raise.

I knew I had been accepted when I was invited with Shirley, another *Norte Americano* (North American), to help make tamales at Nora's home for the church dinner. Shirley and I walked down the dirt track and into Nora's open back door. The cement-block house consisted of two bedrooms that opened off of a central room. This would serve her family of six. This room was furnished with a table along one wall, with a very tired sofa on the opposite wall. Just enough room existed to walk between them. Two mismatched, straight chairs were at the table. A small cabinet held a small color TV tuned to a game show in Spanish.

Across the front of the house, opposite the door we entered, was a narrow room used as a kitchen. Nora had a gas stove, refrigerator, and a sink with running water.

The night before, Nora and her two oldest daughters had boiled eight pounds of chicken in a large enamel pot and had stewed huge, red ancho peppers in another. Three other Mexican ladies joined the group around the table to work. We watched and tried to stay out of the way. They de-boned the chicken and tore the meat into small pieces. The chili peppers were mashed into a puree with water, cumin, salt, and garlic.

Half of this was added to the chicken; both pots were taken back into the kitchen.

Five kilo bags of *masa*—corn flour—were poured into a huge pottery bowl. A handful of salt was added with baking powder; then several blocks of pork fat (lard) and melted pork drippings were kneaded into the *masa* with the chili puree. The ingredients were mixed by hand into a thick paste.

Our teachers demonstrated and giggled as we tried our hand at making tamales. First a wet corn husk was squeezed out and held flat in the left hand. A spoonful of the *masa* was smeared onto the corn husk. If not done with the right pressure and flick of the wrist, the paste came off and ripped the husk. If the paste held, then a large pinch of the chicken mixture was placed down the center of the *masa*. Experienced hands rotated the corn husk, rolled it into a cigar shape, tucked the end over and gently placed it into a steamer. The tamales formed layers of radiating spokes as they filled the steamer. We didn t stay while they cooked, because steaming took several hours.

Shirley and I could better appreciate the work involved and the cost when we helped eat some of the 250 tamales that evening. This dinner was held in an unfinished addition to Pastor Roland's home across the road from his church. In Roland's honor Bonnie had bought a cake, for we were celebrating the pastor's ordination.

The following night's service was interrupted by a dog fight.

Shirley shared her cooking expertise by making jambalaya and crawfish pie. Jack amazed us with his ability and determination to help. We watched with tears as he hoisted a shovel and wheeled himself to a ditch that was being dug for power lines. He maneuvered his wheelchair so he could scrape up small shovelfuls of dirt and lift the dirt out of the ditch.

I recognized many of the people at the different services and children's programs. The kids recognized us as the clowns they had seen before. They smothered us with outstretched hands for balloons. They welcomed us with warm smiles. We responded with friendship and small gifts of clothing and food.

Doing volunteer work was more rewarding than I had ever thought. I came home spiritually rejuvenated and excited about doing whatever I could, whether it was cutting vegetables or cutting out aprons, cooking, cleaning, or clowning. I couldn't wait to see where God would lead next.

Part Six

In Pursuit of a Dream

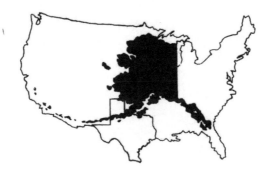

SIXTEEN

In Pursuit of a Dream

Many years before I retired in 1998 from teaching art in public schools, I dreamed of traveling to Alaska. Someday. The dream began to take focus as a real possibility with travel experiences of Jamboree, Tioga, and the Gulfstream named Gus. I started to set goals and began to plan in earnest as retirement neared.

January 2002, I would celebrate birthday number 60 by driving the Alcan Highway, that lonely stretch of road begun the year of my birth (during World War II) to connect the lower 48 with Alaska. Instead of dreading this birthday as a time to reflect and admit to being a "senior citizen", I'd deny aging and encompass freedom and independence. I was overweight and blind without those contact lenses, but otherwise, I was in pretty good health. Alaska here we come!

For a long while I had been checking out travel books from the library. Now I justified buying the best ones over the Internet. I made notes of places that Chris would like to visit and places that were of special interest to me. Lists of everything imaginable covered legal pads.

We would take the Alaskan Marine Highway ferry up the inside passage from Benningham. In order to save money, we had to take the last ferry in April before the summer rates increase in May.

Chris' curriculum was self-paced in workbooks. It was portable; I could Homeschool him. At 12 Chris was an experienced traveler and was old enough to enjoy a long trip without our getting on each others' nerves too much. This trip was do-able, I decided.

One problem existed. If only I could find a way to justify to myself the expenses of the trip. An extended vacation was too selfish. My meager savings would be sorely taxed by self-seeking pleasure.

Finding Mrs. Noah

Before retiring, I was fortunate to be able to be part of The New Jersey Writing Project in the school district and to then train as a writing teacher. Thus inspired, I began my own writing in earnest, both non-fiction and children's books. I experienced the nemesis of rejections, so I began to investigate self-publishing.

The school district printed one of my children's books as part of the writing project. What a mixed blessing to see my words and illustrations as a "real" book! The downside was that I knew nothing about promotion, so the distribution of the book was limited to give-away copies, followed by more rejection of my "serious" work.

Discoveries and questions raised by our trip to Dave's Dino Digs haunted me. I read Creationists' accounts of Noah's Flood, participated in digs at Creation Evidences on the Paluxy River, and read about new discoveries in paleontology. I was disturbed that children were usually presented a fairy-tale version of Noah's Flood and that their most-asked questions about dinosaurs were not answered.

I began to study Creation and Noah in earnest and to write and illustrate for older children a more realistic account of the flood. *Mrs. Noah's Journal* was completed in the winter of 2000. My brother had introduced me to Randy, a printer of gospel tracts and other religious materials. Randy agreed to print my book if I could get the drawings and text perfected by using the Adobe computer programs and a scanner. Now writing was not as much fun. I struggled to teach myself the necessary computer skills.

The book's cover was another major headache, because I could not do the necessary color work my self. Randy had to "job it out". But at last I completed the illustrated text and sent it to him.

While waiting for the books to be printed, I completed a hand-colored copy of the book, designed a costume, and developed a program to present Mrs. Noah and her Journal to groups of children. I made balloon animals for the kids. Six months later I received the first copies of my book.

Mission Service Corps

A delightful, elderly couple from the local Baptist association spoke in our church about the Mission Service Corps. This organization of volunteers, who work in various fields, intrigued me. I inundated the Heiberts with questions. Could this type of volunteer work be in God's plan for me?

In May 2001, Chris and I attended a three-day orientation for the Mission Service Corps at a beautiful conference center on a lake near Dallas. While I attended seminars, Chris was introduced to volunteering. He was asked to help with gardening and happily lent a hand.

Seminars, personal conferences, and interaction with participants and experienced missions volunteers touched that questioning in my heart. Here was a support organization to which I could be accountable.

Yet, I was encouraged to develop my own itinerant ministry through clowning, hosting in resorts or state parks, or in any other way I was led.

Hearing of my desire to volunteer in some way on a trip to Alaska, the orientation leader gave me the name and address of the director of missions in Anchorage. I wrote to him and eagerly waited to receive his reply.

I had been a member of Campers on Mission only by attending a rally and getting on the mailing list. We had not been able to participate in any of this organization's work projects because of my school responsibilities. The 2001 National Campers on Mission was to be held in Rayne, Louisiana, the Frog Capital of the World. I determined to go to the rally and seek out others with ideas for our ministry, and to meet anyone who may have been to Alaska.

The National Rally was a huge success, with 480 participants representing 20 states as far away as New England, California, the Midwest, and of course, Texas. Members from around the nation had donated 442,457 hours of volunteer service. I was impressed by what this organization was doing to help others, whether during disasters, in campgrounds, or building projects.

We parked next to two lovely widows in their 60's who had traveled to this meeting together, even though they usually traveled alone. They were quite an encouragement, telling me about their volunteering experiences. I was invited to join them sightseeing.

I took Chris to Avery Island to visit the Tabasco factory, where we watched the workers bottle hot sauce for Japan as well as for the United States. We received an opportunity to taste different hot sauces and to even buy pepper plants.

Avery Island was maintained as a bird sanctuary, with thousands of cranes, sea birds and tropical plants. We learned about the Arcadian (Cajun) culture and were introduced to Cajun cooking, boudin, crawfish etouffee, and gumbo. I particularly liked a sandwich of fried eggplant, tomatoes, and mozzarella cheese on a seeded bun.

Returning to Rayne, Chris and I hunted for and photographed some of the many frog murals that grace public buildings in the city.

The Cajuns have a great sense of humor and a wonderful dialect that takes some getting used to. I laughed with them as they laughed at themselves. The Cajun attitude and friendliness was an inspiration to me.

I met and talked with several people from Texas Campers on Mission. I was invited to lead a meeting on Alaska at the October Rally of the Campers on Mission of Texas.

The day after our return from the National Rally, the Alaskan Director of missions telephoned that he had received my letter. When he heard about our Campers on Mission (COM) experience, he became excited and asked if I would look into Texas COM partnering with the Alaska COM, which was inactive. I agreed to do what ever I could as a volunteer.

My first real challenge as a Mission Service Corps volunteer occurred on June 11, 2001, when east Houston suffered a devastating flood. My daughter, Cheri, lost her home, as did thousands of others. Her neighborhood received 36 inches of rain in about 12 hours. Floodwaters swept over most of the roads between our homes, but my friend, Brett, was able to get me through to rescue Cheri and her youngest son, Kyle, who had just returned home from having surgery.

On the way to her home Brett stopped to chase a seven-foot-long alligator off the roadway. We passed a flooded yard that had a pickup-truck bed full of goats. The water lapped at the tailgate. Trash and animals swirled past homes with water flowing through the windows. In some cases the water flowed up to the rooftops.

While waiting for the water to recede enough to return to Cheri's home, I worked part-time in local shelters housed in area high-schools gyms. With water receding from buckled floors and soaked furniture, we spent weeks in the steaming heat clearing out her ruined belongings and dragging destroyed furniture, clothing, and personal items to the street for eventual pickup. From daylight to exhaustion we hauled, cleaned, packed, and then began to tear out buckled hardwood floors and mildewed sheetrock. Manual labor had become emotionally satisfying. Exhaustion without pay! I had learned that God uses us in simple, menial ways.

"I consider my life worth nothing to me, if only I may finish the race and complete the task the Lord Jesus has given me" (Acts 20:24).

As I approached 60 and looked back over my life, I realized that God wasn't through with me yet. He had given me the intelligence and motivation to become educated, the compassion to be a parent, and the willingness to follow His directions. Now I look forward to celebrating my 60th birthday by traveling to Alaska as a volunteer laborer for the Lord. What better way to face becoming a senior citizen! I can hardly wait to see where He will lead and how He will provide.

> "But those who hope in the Lord
> will renew their strength;
> They will soar on wings like eagles.
> They will run and not grow weary,
> They will walk and not be faint"
> (Isaiah 40:31).

Appendix A: Glossary

Automatic levelers: built-in hydraulic jacks used when parked

Black water: toilet sewage held in a separate holding tank

Boondocking: camping without hook-ups and camping fee

Cab-over: front section of camper that extends over the driver; used as sleeping space or storage

Class-A motor home: a large, driveable camper built like a bus

Class-B motor home: a van-type camper with conveniences added for living

Class-C motor home: a driveable camper with a bed extending over the cab

Dry camping: without hookups

Dump station: a sewer system in which to empty holding tanks

Full-timing: RVers who live in their campers year around

Gray water: waste water from sinks and shower

Holding tanks: water tanks used to hold waste water

Hookups: refers to connecting water, sewer, and electricity

Inverter: changes battery current into alternating current

Pop-up: a towed camper; its roof is raised for camping

Pull-thru: a campsite that can be driven into and pulled straight out of

Setup: hooking up and leveling at a campsite

Shoreline: a heavy-duty electrical cable that is pulled from the vehicle and plugged into an external power source

Slide-out: a section of some RVs that can be extended to provide additional space

Travel Trailer: non-powered camper, designed to be towed

152

Appendix B: Helpful Resources

Camping Clubs

Best Holiday Trav-L-Park (800) 323-8899
Escapees (409) 327-8873
KOA, Kampgrounds of America (406) 248-7444
CCA, Camper Clubs of America (800) 234-8749
CCC, Coast to Coast (303) 790-CAMP
Good Sam Club (800) 234-3450
Loners of America (314) 322-5548
NACO, National American Corp. (206) 455-3155
ORA, Outdoor Resorts of America (615) 244-5237
RPI, Resort Parks International (800) 635-8498
Thousand Trails, Inc. (206) 455-3155
Yogi Bear's Jellystone Parks (800) 558-2954

Campground Directories

American P.C. Campground Directory, PO Box 820009,
      Dallas, TX 75382-0009 (214) 987-3440.
Anderson's Campground Directory, Drawer 467,
      Lewisburg, WV 24901 (304) 645-1897.
KOA Directory, PO Box 30162, Billings, MT 59107-0162,
      (406) 248-7444.
Little, Mickey, *Camper's Guide to Texas*. (Houston: Gulf
      Publishing, 1990).
Frome, Michael, *National Park Guide* (New York: Prentice
      Hall Travel, 1994).
Trailer Life Campground Directory, TL Enterprises,
      29901 Agoura, CA 91301, (818) 991-4980.
Wheelers RV Guide, Print Media Services, 1310 Jarvis

Ave., Elk Grove Village, IL 60007, (708) 981-0100.
Woodall's Campground Directories, Woodall Publishing. Box
5000, Lake Forest, IL 60045-5000 (800) 323-9076.
Wright, Don, *Guide to Free Campgrounds*, Elkhart, IN,
Cottage Publications, latest edition. 24396 Pleasant
View Dr., Elkhart, IN 46517 (219) 875-8618.
Wright, Don, *Save-A-Buck Camping*, Cottage Publications.
Yogi Bear's *Jellystone Park Directory*, 6201 Kellogg Ave.,
Cincinnati, OH 45228, (513) 232-6800.

Public Lands

Bureau of Land Management (BLM), 1849 C. Street, NW,
Room 5600, Washington, DC 20240, (202) 208-3435.
USDA Forest Service (USFS), PO Box 96090,
Washington, DC 20090, (202) 447-3957.
National Park Service (NPS), (for camping guide, write to:
Government Printing Office, Washington DC 20402-
3925).
US Fish and Wildlife Service, 1849 C Street, NW,
Room 3447, Washington DC 20240, (202) 208-5634.
US Army Corps of Engineers, 3909 Halls Ferry Road,
Vicksburg, MS 39180-6199.

RVing Books

Alderman, Bill, J., and Wilson, Eleanore, *Recreational
Vehicles: Finding the Best Buy* (Chicago: Bonus Books
1989).
Abraham, Marilyn J., *First We Quit Our Jobs* (New York:
Dell Publishing, 1997).
Farlow, Bill, *Professor Farlow's Guide to RVing*,
Snowbirds & Winter Texas Guide,
Freedom Unlimited, Facts of Fulltiming, 101 Rainbow
Dr., #1238, Livingston, TX 77351.

Ford, Norman D., *How to Travel and Get Paid for It*,
(Greenlawn, N.Y.: Harian Publishing, 1970).

Hinkle, S.L., *Camping with the Corps*, Route 2, Box 2460,
Murchison, TX 75778.

Hofmeister, Ron and Barb, *Movin' On* (Livingston, TX:
R & B Publications, 1999).

Moeller, Bill & Jan, *Complete Guide to Full-Time RVing*
(Trailer Life Books, 1998).

Peterson, Joe & Kay, *Home Is Where You Park It*,
The Encyclopedia for RVers.
Travel While You Work, 1996.
The New Survival of the RV Snowbirds, 1997.
Encyclopedia for Rvers, RoVers Publications
Escapees RV Club, Livingston, TX, (888) 757-2582.

Pollard, Ted, *King of the Road*, (Radnor, PA: Remington
Press,1993).

Wright, Don, *How to Buy an RV*,
Guide to Free Camping,
Save-A-Buck, Cottage Publications, 420 South Fourth
St., Elkhart, IN 46516, (800) 272-5518.

RVing Clubs

Americamp, 64 Inverness Dr. East, Englewood, CO
80112-5101, (800) 932-6797.

Coast to Coast Campgrounds, 64 Enverness Drive E.,
Englewood, CO 80112, (800) 368-5721.

Escapees, 100 Rainbow Dr., Livingston, TX 77351,
(409) 327-8873.

Family Motor Coach Assoc., 8291 Clough Pike, Cincinnati,
OH 45244-9976, (800) 543-3622.

Family Travel Trailer Assoc., PO Box 5867, Titusville, FL
327833, (880) 603-1101.

Good Sam Club, PO Box 500, Agoura, CA 91376, (818) 991-4980.

Loners of America, Inc., Rt. 2, Box 85E, Ellsinore, MO 63937-9520, (314) 322-5548.

Loners on Wheels, Inc., PO Box 1355, Poplar Bluff, MO 63901.

RVing Women, Box 82606 Y, Kenmore, WA 98028, (800) 333-9992.

RV Emergency Road Service

Coast to Coast
64 Inverness Dr. E.
Englewood, CO 80112
1-800-368-5721

RRR RV
275 E. Hillcrest Dr., Suite 204
Thousand Oaks, CA 91360
1-800-999-7505

Foremost
Dept. 214, PO Box 3357
Grand Rapids, MI 49501
1-800-237-2060

Road America RV Assistance
3081 Salzedo St.
Coral Cables, FL 33134
1-800-443-4187

Good Sam
PO Box 10205
Des Moines, IA 50380-0205
1-800-234-3450

Travel Guides

Bruno, Susan, & Quaresima, Donna, *An Insiders Guide to Williamsburg, Jamestown-Yorktown* (Manteco, N.C.: Storie/McOwen Publishers, 1987).

Jones, John Oliver, *The U.S. Outdoor Atlas & Recreation Guide*, (Boston: Houghton Mifflin Co., 1992).

Kaye, Evelyn, *Active Woman Vacation Guide*, (Boulder,

CO: Blue Panda Publications, 1997).
Sehlinger, Bob, & Surkiewicz, Joe., *The Unofficial Guide to the Great Smoky & Blue Ridge Region* (New York: Macmillan, 1999).
Slater, Shirley, & Basch, Harry, *Exploring America by RV*, (New York: IDG Books—Frommer's).
Rest Area Guide to U.S. and Canada, American Travel Publications, 6986 El Camino Real, Suite 104-199, Carlsbad, CA 92009, (619) 438-0514.
Texas State Travel Guide, Texas Department of Transportation, Austin, TX.

National Parks
www.nps.gov

Park	Phone Number
Acadia, Maine	(207) 288-3338
Arches, Utah	(435) 719-2299
Badlands, S. Dakota	(605) 433-5361
Big Bend, Texas	(915) 477-2251
Biscayne, Florida	(305) 230-1144
Bryce Canyon, Utah	(435) 834-5322
Canyonlands, Utah	(435) 259-7164
Capitol Reef, Utah	(435) 425-3791
Carlsbad Caverns, N. Mexico	(505) 785-2232
Channel Islands, California	(805) 658-5730
Crater Lake, Oregon	(541) 594-2211
Death Valley, California	(760) 786-2331
Denali, Alaska	(907) 683-2294
Everglades, Florida	(305) 242-7700
Gates of the Actic, Alaska	(907) 456-0281
Glacier, Montana	(406) 888-7800
Glacier Bay, Alaska	(907) 697-2230
Grand Canyon, Arizona	(520) 638-7888
Grand Teton, Wyoming	(307) 739-3300

Great Basin, Nevada	(775) 234-7331
Great Smoky Mountains, Tenn.	(423) 436-1200
Guadalupe Mountains, Texas	(915) 828-3251
Haleakala, Hawaii	(808) 572-4400
Hawaii Volcanoes, Hawaii	(808) 985-6000
Hot Springs, Arkansas	(501) 624-3383
Isle Royal, Michigan	(906) 482-0984
Katmai, Alaska	(907) 246-3305
Kenia Fjords, Alaska	(907) 224-3175
Kobuk Valley, Alaska	(907) 442-3890
Lake Clark, Alaska	(907) 271-3751
Lassen Volcanic, California	(530) 595-4444
Mammoth Cave, Kentucky	(270) 758-2251
Mesa Verde, Colorado	(970) 529-4465
Mount Ranier, Washington	(360) 569-2211
North Cascades, Washington	(360) 856-5700
North Cascades, Washington	(360) 856-5700
Olympic, Washington	(360) 452-4501
Petrified Forest, Arizona	(520) 523-6228
Redwood, California	(707) 464-6101
Rocky Mountain, Colorado	(970) 586-1333
Shenandoah, Virginia	(540) 999-3500
Sequoia & Kings Canyon, California	(559) 565-3341
Theodore Roosevelt, N. Dakota	(701) 623-4466
Virgin Islands, Virgin Islands	(340) 776-6201
Voyageurs, Minnesota	(218) 283-9821
Wind Cave, South Dakota	(605) 745-4600
Wrangell-St. Elias, Alaska	(907) 822-5235
Yosemite, California	(209) 372-0200
Yellowstone, Wyoming	(307) 344-7381
Zion, Utah	(435) 772-3256

Texas State Parks
www.tpwd.state.tx.us
(800) 792-1112
State Tourist Information

State	Office	Web Site
Alabama	(800) 252-2262	touralabama.org
Alaska	(907) 465-2010	travelalaska.com
Arizona	(800) 842-8257	arizonaguide.com
Arkansas	(800) 628-8725	arkansas.com
California	(800) 862-2543	gocalif.com
Colorado	(800) 265-6723	colorado.com
Connecticut	(800) 282-6863	ctbound.org
Delaware	(800) 441-8846	state.de.us
D.C.	(800) 422-8644	washington.org
Florida	(888) 735-2872	flausa.com
Georgia	(800) 847-4842	georgia.org
Hawaii	(800) 464-2924	gohawaii.com
Idaho	(800) 635-7820	visitid.org
Indiana	(800) 289-6646	indianatourism.com
Iowa	(800) 345-4692	state.ia.us/tourism
Kansas	(800) 252-6727	kansas-travel.com
Kentucky	(800) 225-8747	kentuckytourism.com
Louisiana	(800) 695-4064	louisianatravel.com
Maine	(800) 533-9595	visitmaine.com
Maryland	(800) 543-1036	mdisfun.org
Massachusetts	(800) 447-6277	mass-vacation.com
Michigan	(800) 543-2937	michigan.org
Minnesota	(800) 654-3700	exploreminnesota.com
Mississippi	(800) 927-6378	mississippi.org
Missouri	(800) 877-1234	missouritourism.org
Montana	(800) 847-4868	visitmt.com
Nebraska	(800) 228-4307	visitnebraska.org
Nevada	(800) 638-2328	travelnevada.com

New Hampshire	(800) 386-4664	visitnh.gov
New Jersey	(800) 537-7397	state.nj.us/travel
New Mexico	(800) 545-2040	newmexico.org
New York	(800) 225-5697	iloveny.state.ny.us
North Carolina	(800) 847-4862	visitnc.com
North Dakota	(800) 435-5663	ndtourism.com
Ohio	(800) 282-5393	ohiotourism.com
Oklahoma	(800) 652-6552	travelok.com
Oregon	(800) 547-7842	traveloregon.com
Pennsylvania	(800) 847-4872	dced.state.pa.us/visit
Rhode Island	(800) 556-2484	visitrhodeisland.com
South Carolina	(800) 346-3634	travelsc.com
South Dakota	(800) 732-5682	state.sd.us
Tennessee	(800) 836-6200	state.tn.us/tourdev
Texas	(800) 888-8839	traveltex.com
Utah	(800) 200-1160	utah.com
Vermont	(800) 837-6688	travel-vermont.com
Virginia	(800) 527-6517	virginia.org
Washington	(800) 544-1800	experiencewashington.com
West Virginia	(800) 225-5985	callwva.com
Wisconsin	(800) 432-8747	travelwisconsin.com
Wyoming	(800) 225-5996	wyomingtourism.org

Appendix C: Check List

Before Leaving Home

Alert friends and neighbors of your plans.
Arrange to leave a key, itinerary, and contact numbers with a
      trusted friend.
Stop mail and newspapers.
Arrange for someone to water plants, feed pets, mow grass.
Set timers on several lights.
Arrange for police to periodically check on home.
Store valuables in safe place.
Adjust thermostat.
Remove food from refrigerator; empty trash.
Unplug all electrical appliances.
Turn off hot-water heater, water to toilets, and gas to stove.
Inform alarm company.
Lock all windows and doors and set alarm.

In Case of an Emergency

Medical Insurance: _____
Company's phone _____
Policy number _____

Auto Insurance: _____
Agent's number _____

RV Emergency Road Service: _____
Phone number _____
Policy number _____

Important Information

Personal Physician _____   Phone _____

Personal Physician _____   Phone _____

Dentist _____   Phone _____

Relative _____   Phone _____

Neighbor _____   Phone _____

Lawyer _____   Phone _____

Business Office _____   Phone _____

Veterinarian _____   Phone _____

Medical Information

Glasses _____

Contact Lenses _____

Prescriptions _____

Allergies _____

Blood type _____

162

Medical Consent For Unrelated Minor

Whereas, (name) _____ (age, date of birth) _____ is my child, and said child is traveling with (name of responsible adult) _____ on a trip from (date) _____ to (date)_____

It is my desire and intent to ensure that said child will receive any necessary medical treatment, and I authorize the named adult accompanying my child to consent to the rendering of such treatment in the event that I cannot be reached. Therefore, I do hereby convey to (name of responsible adult) _____, authority to procure and consent to emergency medical care for my child, including medication or surgery, while my child is in the custody of the adult mentioned above and all reasonable attempts have been made to contact me.

My child _____ is known to have (disease or condition) _____ and is on prescribed medication _____ dosage _____
He/she is allergic to the following _____

Our family doctor is _____ Phone _____

I give permission for my child to be given Tylenol, Pepto-Bismol, cough drops, _____ if needed.

Parent's signature _____ Date _____
Home phone _____ Work phone _____
Cell phone _____

Before Starting the Engine

Plan itinerary and mark route.
Update travel log with mileage and camping information.
Walk around vehicle.
Thump tires.
Wipe headlights, windshield, outside mirrors.
Make sure sewer hose and shore lines are properly stored.
Outside steps are up.
Close any open windows.
Check holding tank levels, water level, gas (or diesel), propane
   (LP).
Reset refrigerator.
Turn off water pump.
Turn off AC/heater.
Lower TV antenna and secure TV.
Lock doors.
Adjust mirrors.
Fasten seatbelts.
Have a great day!

Appendix D: Camp Cooking

Open-Fire Cooking
The trick to starting a good campfire is to have plenty of fuel on hand. In a fire ring or cleared area of dirt, lay a fine layer of tinder (pine needles, dry grass, or dryer lint). Build a teepee of thin kindling (dry sticks, no thicker than a pencil, that form a raised, inverted cone over the tinder). Add thicker sticks loosely over the kindling, leaving plenty of space for air circulation. Light the tinder, blowing or fanning to help ignite. As the small twigs begin to burn, gradually add larger sticks. If adding charcoal, add a few pieces at a time so you won't smother the fire.

Biscuit on a Stick
Scrape the bark off a long green stick. Make basic biscuit dough from dry mix. Knead dough into a long, thick roll and wrap the dough around the stick, beginning at one end and winding it down, sealing the end and edges together. Bake over coals until dough is browned. Carefully remove cooked bread from stick. Fill the center with butter, jelly, or honey.

S'Mores
Skewer marshmallows on a long stick. Heat until toasted. Sandwich marshmallows with squares of chocolate between graham crackers.

Baked in the Coals
Wrap washed, unpeeled potatoes in several layers of foil. Place in coals; turn over occasionally until soft. Core apples. Stuff center with butter, brown sugar, and raisins. Wrap in foil. Bake in coals. Make a slit in the curve of an unpeeled banana. Open the slit and insert squares of chocolate. Wrap banana in foil and bake.

Silver Turtles
Silver turtles are meals in one. On a doubled sheet of foil place
a piece of boneless chicken (or hamburger patty, sausage, etc.)
potato slices, onion slices, and carrot strips. Add salt and pepper. Wrap foil tightly; place in coals for 10 minutes. Turn over
for another 10 minutes or more.

Dutch-Oven Cooking
As a Girl Scout I learned Dutch-oven cooking. Then as a Boy-
Scout leader I relearned it. I found an old, rusty, legless Dutch
oven made for a wood-burning stove and bought a new one with
three legs and a flanged lid. A few cookbooks got me started. I
scrubbed the rust and crud off the old one and washed both with
hot, soapy water, rinsed them well, and dried them in a warm
oven. Pots and lids were seasoned by rubbing inside and out
with vegetable oil and heated in a 350-degree oven for 20 minutes. I turned off the oven and left them inside until cool. I use
the flat-bottom one in my oven and the other over a fire. They
cook equally well.

How to Light a Charcoal Fire
The easiest way to start a charcoal fire is in a charcoal chimney.
These can be purchased or made from a #10 can. Remove both
ends of the can. Using a punch-type opener, punch holes around
the rim on one end. Wad a 12-inch square of chicken wire into
the end of the can with the holes. The wire should be just above
the holes and should fill about one fourth of the can. Punch two
holes opposite each other at the opposite rim. Add a coat hanger wire through these holes for a handle.

To use, lightly wad a sheet of newspaper (or dryer lint) into the
can on top of the wire. Add charcoal to almost fill the can. Light
the newspaper from the bottom. Air entering the holes feeds the
fire, which will light and heat the charcoal. When the charcoal
is white-hot, it can be placed in the fire ring or on base of a grill.

Use hot charcoal under and on top of a Dutch oven. Use the lid of the Dutch oven as a frying pan on the grill. For breakfast try Toad-in-a-Hole. Tear a hole in the center of a slice of bread. Heat butter in fry pan. Toast one side of bread. Break an egg into the hole; cook until set. Turn the bread over with the egg; toast the other side.

Boy-Scout Cobbler
An all-time favorite. Open one large can or two small cans of any flavor pie filling. Dump into Dutch oven. Shake a box of dry cake mix evenly over the pie filling. Top with dabs of butter. Top with lid. Place Dutch oven over 10-12 hot charcoal briquettes. Space 10-12 briquettes on the lid. Leave it alone for about 20 minutes or until the fragrance is impossible to ignore. Great combinations are: peach pie flling and yellow cake mix, apple pie filling and spice cake, cherry pie filling and chocolate cake. Ummm!

Chicken Pie
From dry mix, mix up a double recipe of biscuits. Press half of the biscuit dough onto the bottom and sides of the Dutch oven. Mix one 10-ounce can of chicken, one 10-ounce can of mixed vegetables, and one can of cream of mushroom or cream of celery soup. Pour mixture onto biscuit crust. Pat out remaining biscuit dough and place on top of mixture. Crimp crusts together. Bake for 20 minutes on 10-12 briquettes with 10-12 on top.

Chicken and Dumplings
Heat a little oil in Dutch oven. Brown two pounds of chicken thighs in oil. When chicken is browned, add one large can of mixed vegetables and two packages of cream of chicken gravy mix. Mix one batch of biscuit dough. Drop spoonfuls of the biscuit mix around the top of the chicken mixture. Push the dough down. Place on the lid. Bake for about 30 minutes on 14 coals with 8-10 coals on top.

Chili Pie
Empty a couple of cans of chili into a Dutch oven. Prepare a package of cornbread mix, pour over chili, top with shredded Cheddar cheese. Add the lid and bake 10-15 minutes until the cornbread is done.

Mexican Chicken
In Dutch oven, sauté one chopped onion in 1/2 stick melted butter. Add a small can of mushrooms, one can cream of mushroom soup, and 1/2 pound pasteurized process cheese loaf, cut in pieces. Cook over low heat, stirring constantly until cheese melts and becomes a sauce. Rmove from coals. Crush one large bag of tortilla chips and mix most of the chips with sauce and two large cans of chicken. Top with remaining chips. Add lid and bake for 30 minutes on top of 8-10 coals.

Roast and Veggies
Using a hot Dutch oven, brown in oil a cheap cut of roast. Remove roast. Brown onion and garlic to taste. Return meat to the oven. Add a small amount of water. Add lid. Simmer over coals for several hours. Slow cooking will insure tender meat. Lid will form a vacuum, so use caution when removing. When meat is tender, add cut-up potatoes and carrots. Simmer with lid for 10-20 minutes.

Crawfish Etouffee (From Rayne, Louisiana)
Melt one stick of butter in hot Dutch oven. Stir in 1/2 cup of flour; brown lightly. Add one bell pepper, two medium onions, and three cloves of garlic, all diced. Add one cup of water; cook uncovered for one hour adding 1/2 cup of water if necessary. Add 1 1/2 pounds of crawfish tails, salt, red and black pepper, and some chopped green-onion tops. Simmer for 20 minutes. Serve over steamed rice.

168

Alligator Chili (Boy Scout, Scout Fair)
Brown in olive oil one pound of ground alligator tail. Add one diced onion, three cans of diced tomatoes, 4 4-ounce cans diced chilies, one 52-ounce can Ranch-style beans, and 1/4 cup red chili powder. Simmer 1-2 hours.

Rancher's Breakfast
In Dutch oven brown one pound bulk sausage. Add two or three cubed potatoes and chopped onion to taste. Stir until potatoes are soft. Add six or more whole eggs; scramble together. Serve on warm tortillas with shredded Cheddar cheese and salsa.

King of England Biscuits (Boy Scout, Scout Fair)
This historic, scratch biscuit recipe traces its origins to the Warren Plantation along the James River in Early Virginia, long before the American Revolution. It has been used for more than 300 years and was fed to soldiers during the Revolution and the Civil War. Cowboys prepared these biscuits up the Chisholm, Loving, and Goodnight Trails. These biscuits were fed to the King of England by Houston Boy-Scout Preston Weatherred Jr., during the 1929 World Jamboree in Birkenhead, England. They are said to have been royally approved, thus their name.

For each person served:
One handful of flour
One pinch of salt
Two pinches of soda
One tablespoon of lard or shortening

Mix well and add buttermilk until dough has the consistency of clay. Bake in a covered Dutch oven for 20 minutes. Best served warm with homemade preserves and butter.

Funnel Cake
Another fun recipe. Beat two eggs. Add 1 2/3 cups of milk. Sift together two cups plain flour, one teaspoon baking powder, 1/2 teaspoon salt, and one tablespoon sugar. Add to dry ingredients the milk and egg mixture. Mix well. Add a little extra milk to make mixture thinner than pancake batter. In Dutch oven heat one inch of oil until slightly bubbling. Dribble batter through a funnel and into hot oil. Turn once. Remove to paper towel; sprinkle with powdered sugar.

How to Clean a Burned Dutch Oven
Usually a Dutch oven can be cleaned by simply wiping it out with paper towels. But sometimes. . . ..
Scrape out burned bits with a wooden or plastic (not metal) spoon. Heat water in the pot until it boils. Scrape off the burned crust as it loosens. Rinse out. You may use a plastic pot scrubber. Soap is not necessary. If you must use soap, then you will have to re-season the pot. Store with paper inside to absorb moisture. If oven appears rusty after storage, simply wash well with warm water, lightly oil, and dry thoroughly on the fire or in an oven.

Cookbooks

Log Cabin Campfire Cooking', 900 E. Carnation Dr., Sandy, UT, 884094.

Good Sam RV Cookbook, Good Sam Club, PO Box 500, Agoura, CA 91376.

Woodall's Campsite Cookbook (Lake Forest, IL: Woodall Publishing).

Woodall's Favorite Recipes from America's Campgrounds, Woodall Publishing.

Clahan, Zock, *Dining with Zock, A Complete Guide to RV/Tailgate Cooking*, PO Box 16157, Encino, CA. 91416.

Mulls, Shelia, *The Outdoor Dutch Oven Cookbook*, (Maine: Ragged Mountain Press, 1997).

Ragsdale, John G., *Camper's Guide to Outdoor Cooking*, (Houston: Gulf Publishing, 1989).

Ragsdale, John G., *Dutch Oven Cooking* (Houston: Gulf Publishing, 1997).

Ryan, Joyce, *The Happy Camper's Gourmet Cookbook*, Butterfly Books, San Antonio, TX 78247.

How to order more copies of

Grandma's on the Go

and obtain a free Hannibal Books catalog
FAX: 1-972-487-7960
Call: 1-800-747-0738 (in Texas, 1-972-487-5710)
Email: orders@hannibalbook.com
Mail copy of form below to:
Hannibal Books
P.O. Box 461592
Garland, Texas 75046
Visit: www.hannibalbooks.com

Number of copies desired _____
Multiply number of copies by $9.95   ___X___$9.95___
Cost of books: $_____

Please add $3 for postage and handling for first book and add 50-cents for each additional book in the order.
Shipping $_____
Texas residents add 8.25 % sales tax $_____

Total order $_____

Mark method of payment: check enclosed _____
Credit card# _____ exp. date_____
(Visa, MasterCard, Discover, American Express accepted)

Name _____

Address _____

City State, Zip _____

Phone _____ FAX _____

Email _____

These missions books are also available

Rescue by Jean Phillips. American missionaries Jean Phillips and husband Gene lived through some of the most harrowing moments in African history of the last half century. Abducted and threatened with death, Jean and Gene draw on God's lessons of a lifetime.

_____Copies at $12.95=_____

Beyond Surrender by Barbara J. Singerman. After surrendering to missions in Benin, Barbara Singerman and her family found that the only similarity between themselves and the Beninese that they all walk upright on two feet and smile. Why serve in a place where major diseases stalked their lives, where accomplishing basic, daily tasks caused unthinkable fatigue? The answer came in the desperate plea of villagers, "Please come back and tell us more about Jesus."

_____Copies at $12.95=_____

Unmoveable Witness by Marion Corley. An alarming interrogation by Colombia's version of the FBI. A dangerous mishap at a construction site. A frightening theft at his home in Bucaramanga, Colombia. What kept Marion and Evelyn Corley on the mission field for 22 years when others might have returned to Stateside comforts?

_____Copies at $9.95=_____

Awaken the Dawn by Doris B. Wolfe. Christian romance novel set in the jungles of South America involving two missionaries, one a recent widower with two children and the other a young, never-married single woman. He's a pilot. She's a teacher. Dramatic real-life situations test their faith.

_____Copies at $9.95=_____

Add $3.00 shipping for first book, plus 50-cents for each additional book.

Shipping & Handling _____

Texas residents add 8.25% sales tax _____

TOTAL ENCLOSED_____

check _____ or credit card # _____ exp. date_____

(Visa, MasterCard, Discover, American Express accepted)

Name _____

Address _____ Phone _____

City _____ State _____ Zip _____

Email _____

For postal address, phone number, fax number, email address and other ways to order from Hannibal Books, see page 173